Karen Brown's
ENGLAND

Charming Bed & Breakfasts

Written by
JUNE BROWN

Illustrations by Barbara Tapp
Cover Painting by Jann Pollard

Karen Brown's Country Inn Series

Karen Brown Titles

Austria: Charming Inns & Itineraries

California: Charming Inns & Itineraries

England: Charming Bed & Breakfasts

England, Wales & Scotland: Charming Hotels & Itineraries

France: Charming Bed & Breakfasts

France: Charming Inns & Itineraries

Germany: Charming Inns & Itineraries

Ireland: Charming Inns & Itineraries

Italy: Charming Bed & Breakfasts

Italy: Charming Inns & Itineraries

Portugal: Charming Inns & Itineraries

Spain: Charming Inns & Itineraries

Switzerland: Charming Inns & Itineraries

Dedicated with All My Love

to My Parents

Gladys & George

Dear Fran,
Best wishes and a happy retirement.
My personal thanks for the opportunity
to work with you and for your
care and concern for
all of us.
You will be missed
Sincerely
Kate

The painting on the front cover is Selworthy, Somerset

Editors: Karen Brown, June Brown, Clare Brown, Kim Brown Holmsen, Iris Sandilands, Gretchen DeAndre.

Illustrations: Barbara Tapp; Cover painting: Jann Pollard.

Maps: Susanne Lau Alloway—Greenleaf Design & Graphics; Back cover photo: William H. Brown.

Copyright © 1988, 1993, 1995, 1996, 1997, 1998 by Karen Brown's Guides.

This book or parts thereof may not be reproduced in any form without obtaining written permission from the publisher: Karen Brown's Guides, P.O. Box 70, San Mateo, CA 94401, USA, email: karen@karenbrown.com.

Distributed by Fodor's Travel Publications, Inc., 201 East 50th Street, New York, NY 10022, USA.

Distributed in the United Kingdom by Random House UK, 20 Vauxhall Bridge Road, London, SW1V 2SA, phone: 44 171 973 9000, fax: 44 171 840 8408.

Distributed in Australia by Random House Australia, 20 Alfred Street, Milsons Point, Sydney NSW 2061, Australia, phone: 61 2 9954 9966, fax: 61 2 9954 4562.

Distributed in New Zealand by Random House New Zealand, 18 Poland Road, Glenfield, Auckland, New Zealand, phone: 64 9 444 7197, fax: 64 9 444 7524.

Distributed in South Africa by Random House South Africa, Endulani, East Wing, 5A Jubilee Road, Parktown 2193, South Africa, phone: 27 11 484 3538, fax: 27 11 484 6180.

A catalog record for this book is available from the British Library.

Library of Congress Cataloging-in-Publication Data

Brown, June, 1949-
    Karen Brown's England : charming bed & breakfasts / written by
June Brown ; illustrations by Barbara Tapp ; cover painting by Jann
Pollard. -- Totally rev. 7th ed.
      p. cm. -- (Karen Brown's country inn series)
    Includes index.
    ISBN 0-930328-67-1 (pb.)
    1. Bed and breakfast accommodations--England--Guidebooks.
2. England--Guidebooks.   I. Brown, Karen, 1956- . II. Title.
III. Series.
TX907.5.G7B76   1997
647.9442'03--dc21   97-11561
                                                   CIP

Contents

Introduction

Lower Slaughter

England: Charming Bed & Breakfasts describes special accommodations in tranquil countryside locations, picturesque villages, historic towns, and a selection of cultural cities beyond London. Interspersed with thatched cottages and grand ancestral manors are traditional pubs and guesthouses—all offering wholehearted hospitality in charming surroundings. Every place to stay is one that we have seen and enjoyed—our personal recommendation. We sincerely believe that where you lay your head each night makes the difference between a good and a great vacation. If you prefer to travel the hotel route, or are looking for itinerary suggestions, we trust you'll find just what you need in our companion guide, *England, Wales & Scotland: Charming Hotels & Itineraries*.

About Bed and Breakfast Travel

Every place to stay in this book has a different approach to bed and breakfast. Some households are very informal, some welcome children, and others invite you to sample gracious living, cocktails in the drawing room, billiards after dinner, and croquet on the lawn. The one thing that they have in common is a warmth of welcome. We have tried to be candid and honest in our appraisals and tried to convey each listing's special flavor so that you know what to expect and will not be disappointed. To help you appreciate and understand what to expect when staying at places in this guide, the following pointers are given in alphabetical order, not order of importance.

ANIMALS

Even if animals are not mentioned in the write-up, the chances are that there are friendly, tail-wagging dogs and sleek cats as visible members of the families. Many listings accept their guests pets.

ARRIVAL AND DEPARTURE

Always discuss your time of arrival—hosts usually expect you to arrive around 6 pm. If you are going to arrive late or early, be certain to telephone your host. You are generally expected to leave by 10 am on the morning of your departure. By and large you are not expected to be on the premises during the day.

BATHROOMS

In the listing we state how many rooms have en-suite bathrooms in the bedrooms. Several listings have private bathrooms which means that your facilities are located down the hall.

BEDROOMS

Beds are often made with duvets (down comforters) instead of the more traditional blankets and sheets. A double room has one double bed, a twin room has two single beds, and a family room contains one or more single beds in addition to a double bed. Zip and link beds are very popular: these are twin beds that can be zipped together (linked) to form an American queen-sized bed. American king and queen beds are still few and far between.

CHILDREN

Places that welcome children state "Children welcome." The majority of listings in this guide do not "welcome" children but find they become tolerable at different ages over 5 or, more often than not, over 12. In some cases places simply do not accept children and the listing states "Children not accepted." However, these indications of children's acceptability are not cast in stone, so if you have your heart set on staying at a listing that accepts children over 12 and you have an 8-year-old, call them, explain your situation, and they may well take you. Ideally, we would like to see all listings welcoming children and all parents remembering that they are staying in a home and doing their bit by making sure that children do not run wild.

CHRISTMAS

Several listings offer Christmas getaways. If the information section indicates that the listing is open during the Christmas season, there is a very good chance that it offers a festive Christmas package.

CREDIT CARDS

The majority of places in this guide do not accept plastic payment. If the accommodation accepts payment by credit card, it is indicated using the terms AX—American Express, MC—MasterCard, VS—Visa, or simply, all major.

DIRECTIONS

We give concise driving directions to guide you to the listing which is often in a more out-of-the-way place than the town or village in the address. We would be very grateful if you would let us know of cases where our directions have proved inadequate.

ELECTRICITY

The voltage is 240. Most bathrooms have razor points (American-style) for 110 volts. It is recommended that overseas visitors take only dual-voltage appliances and a kit of electrical plugs. Often your host can loan you a hairdryer or an iron.

Castleton

Introduction—About Bed & Breakfast Travel

MAPS

At the back of the book is a key map of Great Britain plus six regional maps showing the location of the town or village nearest the lodging. To make it easier for you, we have divided each location map into a grid of four parts, a, b, c, and d, as indicated on each map's key. The pertinent regional map number is given at the right on the top line of each bed and breakfast's description. These maps are an artist's renderings are not intended to replace commercial maps: our suggestion is to purchase a large-scale road atlas of England where an inch equals 10 miles. Our maps can be cross-referenced with those in our companion guide, *England, Wales & Scotland: Charming Hotels & Itineraries*.

MEALS

Prices quoted always include breakfast. Breakfast is most likely to be juice, a choice of porridge (oatmeal) or cereal, followed by a plate of egg, bacon, sausage, tomatoes, and mushrooms completed by toast, marmalade, and jams—all accompanied by tea or coffee. A great many places offer evening meals which should be requested at the time you make your reservation. You cannot expect to arrive at a bed and breakfast and receive dinner if you have not made reservations for it several days in advance. At some homes the social occasion of guests and host gathered around the dining-room table for an evening dinner party is a large part of the overall experience and many of these types of listings expect their guests to dine in. Places that do not offer evening meals are always happy to make recommendations for guests at nearby pubs or restaurants.

RATES

Rates are those quoted to us for the 1998 summer season. We have tried to standardize rates by quoting the 1998 per person bed-and-breakfast rate based on two people occupying a room. Not all places conform, so where dinner is included we have stated this in the listing. Prices are always quoted to include breakfast, Value Added Tax (VAT), and service (if these are applicable). Please use the figures printed as a guideline and be certain to ask what the rate is at the time of booking. Prices for a single are usually higher than the per-person rates and prices for a family room are sometimes lower. Many listings offer special terms, below their normal prices, for "short breaks" of two or more nights. In several listings suites are available at higher prices.

RESERVATIONS

Reservations can be confining and usually must be guaranteed by a deposit: however, if you have your heart set on a particular place, to avoid disappointment make a reservation. If you prefer to travel as whim and the weather dictate, rooms can often be had in the countryside with just a few days' notice. July and August are the busiest times and if you are traveling to a popular spot such as Bath or York, it is advisable to make reservations. It is completely unacceptable practice to make reservations for a particular night at several establishments, choosing at the last minute which one to stay at.

Although proprietors do not always strictly adhere to it, it is important to understand that once reservations are confirmed, whether by phone or in writing, you are under contract. This means that the proprietor is legally obligated to provide the accommodation he has promised and that you are bound to pay for that accommodation. If you cannot take up your accommodation, you are liable for a portion of the accommodation charges plus your deposit. If you have to cancel your reservation, do so as soon as possible so that the proprietor can attempt to re-let your room in which case you are liable only for the re-let fee or the deposit.

If you are visiting from overseas, our preference for making a reservation is by telephone: the cost is minimal and you have your answer immediately, so if space is not available, you can then decide on an alternative. If calling from the United States, allow for the time difference—England is five hours ahead of New York—so that you can call during their business day. Dial 011 (the international code), 44 (Britain's code), then the city code (dropping the 0), and the telephone number. Be specific as to what your needs are, such as a ground-floor room, en-suite bathroom, or twin beds. Check the prices which may well have changed from those given in the book (summer 1998). Ask what deposit to send or give your credit card number. Tell them about what time you intend to arrive and request dinner if you want it. Ask for a confirmation letter with brochure and map to be sent to you. Faxing is an excellent way to get a quick response in "black and white." In any written communication with England, do spell out the month since they reverse the American month/day numbering system—for example, to the English, 9/12 means December 9th, not September 12th.

SIGHTSEEING

We have tried to mention major sightseeing attractions near each lodging to encourage you to spend several nights in each location since few countries have as much to offer in a concentrated space as England. Within a few miles of every listing there are places of interest to visit and explore: lofty cathedrals, quaint churches, museums, and grand country houses.

SMOKING

Nearly all listings forbid smoking either in the bedrooms or public rooms. Some allow no smoking at all, in which case we state "No-smoking house." Ask about smoking policies if this is important to you—best to be forewarned rather than frustrated.

Kersey

Introduction—About Bed & Breakfast Travel

SOCIALIZING

We have tried to indicate the degree of socializing that is included in your stay as some hosts treat their guests like visiting friends and relatives, sharing cocktails, eating with them around the dining-room table, and joining them for coffee after dinner (the difference being that friends and relatives do not receive a bill at the end of their stay).

WOLSEY LODGES

Several of the listings are members of Wolsey Lodges, a consortium of private houses that open their doors to a handful of guests at a time. Visitors become a part of the household—guests are not expected to scuttle up to their rooms and family life does not carry on away from guests behind closed doors. Everyone usually dines together round a polished table, and unless you make special requests, you eat what is served to you. The conversation flows and you meet those you might never have met elsewhere. Early or late in the season, you may find that you are the only guests in these houses and you can enjoy a romantic candlelit dinner in a house full of character and charm. You are welcome as guests because you are the ones who help the owners pay their central heating bills, private school fees, and gardeners. As with all the listings in this guide, Wolsey Lodge members approach bed and breakfast in different ways—some are informal, while others offer a taste of refined, gracious living. If a lodging is a member of this group, we state "Wolsey Lodge" in the information section. A brochure listing all the Wolsey Lodge properties is available from Wolsey Lodges, 9 Market Place, Hadleigh, Ipswich, Suffolk IP7 5DL, England, tel: (01473) 822058, fax: (01473) 827444.

About England

DRIVING

Just about the time overseas visitors board their return flight home, they will have adjusted to driving on the "right" side which is the left side in England. You must contend with such things as roundabouts (circular intersections); flyovers (overpasses); ring roads (peripheral roads whose purpose is to bypass city traffic); lorries (trucks); laybys (turn outs); boots (trunks); and bonnets (hoods). Pedestrians are permitted to cross the road anywhere and always have the right of way. Seat belts must be worn at all times.

Motorways: The letter "M" precedes these convenient ways to cover long distances. With three or more lanes of traffic either side of a central divider, you should stay in the left-hand lane except for passing. Motorway exits are numbered and correspond to numbering on major road maps. Service areas supply petrol, cafeterias, and "bathrooms" (the word "bathroom" is used in the American sense—in Britain "bathroom" means a room with a shower or bathtub, not a toilet: "loo" is the most commonly used term for an American bathroom).

"A" Roads: The letter "A" precedes the road number. All major roads fall into this category. They vary from three lanes either side of a dividing barrier to single carriageways with an unbroken white line in the middle indicating that passing is not permitted. These roads have the rather alarming habit of changing from dual to single carriageway.

"B" Roads and Country Roads: The letter "B" preceding the road number or the lack of any lettering or numbering indicate that it belongs to the maze of country roads that crisscross Britain. These are the roads for people who have the luxury of time to enjoy the scenery en route. Arm yourself with a good map (although getting lost is part of the fun). Driving these narrow roads is terrifying at first but exhilarating after a while. Meandering down these roads, you can expect to spend time crawling behind a tractor or cows being herded to the farmyard. Some lanes are so narrow that there is room for only one car.

INFORMATION

The British Tourist Authority is an invaluable source of information. Their major offices are located as follows:

AUSTRALIA–SYDNEY: BTA, Level 16, Gateway, 1 Macquarie Place, Sydney NWS 2000, tel: (02) 9377 4400, fax: (02) 9377 4499

CANADA–TORONTO: BTA, 111 Avenue Road, Suite 450, Toronto, Ontario M5R 3J8, tel: (888) VISITUK, fax: (416) 961-2175

FRANCE–PARIS: BTA, Maison de la Grand Bretagne, 19 Rue des Mathurins, 75009 Paris, tel: (1) 4451 5620, fax: (1) 4451 5621

GERMANY–FRANKFURT: BTA, Taunusstrasse 52-60, 60329 Frankfurt, tel: (069) 238 0711, fax: (069) 238 0717

NEW ZEALAND–AUCKLAND: BTA, Suite 305, 3rd Floor, Dilworth Building, corner Queen and Customs Streets, Auckland 1, tel: (09) 303 1446, fax: (09) 377 6965

USA–CHICAGO: BTA, 625 North Michigan Avenue, Suite 1510, Chicago, IL 60611—walk-in inquiries only

USA–NEW YORK: BTA, 551 Fifth Avenue, New York, NY 10176, tel: (800) 462-2748 or in NY (212) 986-2200

If you need additional information while you are in Britain, there are more than 700 official Tourist Information Centers identified by a blue-and-white letter "I" and "Tourist Information" signs. Many information centers will make reservations for local accommodation and larger ones will "book a bed ahead" in a different locality.

In London at the British Travel Centre at 12 Lower Regent Street, London SW1Y 4PQ (near Piccadilly Circus tube station) you can book a room, hire a car, or pay for a coach tour or theatre tickets. It is open 9 am to 6:30 pm, Monday to Friday; 10 am to 4 pm Saturday and Sunday, with extended hours from mid-May to September.

PUBS

Pubs are a British institution. Traditional pubs with inviting names such as the Red Lion, Wheatsheaf, and King's Arms are found at the heart of every village. Not only are they a great place to meet the locals over a pint or a game of dominoes or darts, but they offer an inviting place to dine. Food served in the bar enables you to enjoy an inexpensive meal while sipping your drink in convivial surroundings. Bar meals range from a bowl of soup to a delicious cooked dinner. Many pubs have dining rooms that serve more elaborate fare in equally convivial but more sophisticated surroundings. The key to success when dining at a pub is to obtain a recommendation from where you are staying that night—your host is always happy to assist you.

Introduction—About England

SHOPPING

None EU members can reclaim the VAT (Value Added Tax) that they pay on the goods they purchase. Not all stores participate in the refund scheme and there is often a minimum purchase price. Stores that do participate will ask to see your passport before completing the VAT form. This form must be presented with the goods to the Customs officer at the point of departure from Britain within three months of purchase. The customs officer will certify the form. After having the receipts validated by customs you can receive a refund in cash from the tax-free refund counter. Alternately you can mail your validated receipts to the store where you bought the goods. The store will then send you a check in sterling for the refund.

SIGHTSEEING

There is so much to see in every little nook and cranny of England: cottage gardens, Roman ruins, stately homes, thatched villages, ancient castles, Norman churches, smugglers' inns, bluebell woods, historic manors, museums on every subject. All set in a land that moves from wild moorland to verdant farmland, woodland to meadow, vast sandy beaches to rugged cliffs. Most sightseeing venues operate a summer and a winter opening schedule, the changeover occurring around late March/early April and late October/early November. Before you embark on an excursion, check the dates and hours of opening. The British Tourist Authority is an invaluable resource for what to see and do in an area. Our companion guide, *England, Wales & Scotland: Charming Hotels & Itineraries,* includes countryside driving itineraries which are useful in helping you plan your holiday.

WEATHER

Britain has a tendency to be moist at all times of the year. The cold in winter is rarely severe; however, the farther north you go, the greater the possibility of being snowed in. Spring can be wet, but it is a lovely time to travel—the summer crowds have not descended, daffodils and bluebells fill the woodlands, and the hedgerows are full of wildflowers. Summer offers the best chance of sunshine, but also the largest crowds. Schools are usually closed the last two weeks of July and all of August, so this is the time when most families take their summer holidays. Travel is especially hectic on the weekends in summer—try to avoid major routes and airports at these times. Autumn is also an ideal touring time. The weather tends to be drier than in spring and the woodlands are decked in their golden autumn finery.

St. Michael's Mount

Introduction—About England

Bed & Breakfast Descriptions

The Benedictine monks chose a magnificent site high on a hill overlooking the sea to found their Abbey of St Peter in 1024. Despite having been sacked by Henry VIII and burned by Cromwell, a lot of the monastic settlement remains: the church, the magnificent swannery, an enormous thatched tithe barn, a ruined watermill, and most importantly the infirmary. Now home to the Cookes, the infirmary was originally a resting-place for visitors, evolving over the years into a farmhouse and now a welcoming guest house and tea-rooms. Pink chairs with tables topped with pink cloths are set around the giant inglenook fireplace in the old kitchen. Breakfast and lunch are served here or, on warm summer days, under the vine-covered arbor or on the lawn overlooking the barn. Bedrooms range in size from a spacious suite with a sitting room and separate bedroom to a cottagey little room set beneath the eaves and reached by a narrow staircase. The adjacent tithe barn contains interesting exhibits while the farm with its array of animals is a great attraction to young visitors as is the nearby swannery with its vast colony of swans. Abbotsbury is a delightful village of thatched houses very typical of those found just a short drive away in Hardy country, a favorite destination for visitors. *Directions:* Abbotsbury is midway between Weymouth and Bridport on the B3157. In Abbotsbury turn towards the sea (signposted The Swannery) and Abbey House is on your left after 100 yards.

ABBEY HOUSE   New
Owners: Maureen & Jonathan Cooke
Church Street
Abbotsbury, Dorset DT3 4JJ, England
Tel: (01305) 871330, Fax: (01305) 871088
5 rooms, 4 en suite
£30 per person
Open all year, Credit cards: none
Children welcome, No-smoking house

The Old Vicarage offers visitors an exceptionally delightful place to stay in this tranquil part of the country immortalized in Thomas Hardy's novels. Standing next to the old village church, surrounded by green lawns, neatly clipped hedges, and rose gardens, this fine Georgian house is owned by Anthea and Michael Hipwell who, along with their black labrador Beeze, offer a warm welcome to their gracious home. Breakfast is the only meal that Anthea prepares, but she has a long list of wonderful restaurants in the surrounding villages. Upstairs, the bedrooms have pretty wallpapers and are furnished in tasteful English country style, in character with the decor throughout The Old Vicarage. There is a lot to see and do in the area: Cerne Abbas is a particularly attractive village of thatched cottages and has a giant carved into the hillside. Salisbury, Shaftesbury, and the Casterbridge of Hardy's novels, historic Dorchester, are nearby. The Dorset coast (Lulworth Cove, Durdle Door, and Ringstead Bay) is a 20-minute drive away. *Directions:* From Dorchester take the A35 northeast for 5 miles to Tolpuddle (this is the village where the six martyrs met to fight starvation farmworkers' wages) where you turn right for Affpuddle (1 mile).

THE OLD VICARAGE
Owners: Anthea & Michael Hipwell
Affpuddle
Dorchester
Dorset DT2 7HH, England
Tel & fax: (01305) 848315
www.karenbrown.com/england/theold vicarage .html
3 rooms, 2 en suite
£22.50–£25 per person, dinner approx £10
Closed Christmas to New Year, Credit cards: none
Children over 10

Sheila and Tony Sutton have converted this impressive house, which was built as a vicarage in 1869, into a small hotel providing a centrally located, comfortable, hospitable base for exploring the Lake District. Bric-a-brac, capacious sofas, and an aspidistra in the window give a cluttered, Victorian air to the front lounge, though I would term the overall decor comfortably eclectic. Accommodation can be taken on a bed and breakfast basis, but guests usually opt for the dinner, bed-and-breakfast rate because the Suttons make every effort to make dinner a special occasion. A typical menu might include warm smoked trout mousse with watercress and lemon, guinea fowl with walnuts and mushrooms, sticky toffee pudding, and cheese. Grey Friar is just a short distance from the bustling center of Ambleside. Whether you explore Lakeland by car or on foot, you will find the scenery glorious: in spring the famous daffodils bloom, while in autumn the bracken and leaves turn a crisp, golden brown. At nearby Grasmere are Rydal Mount and Dove Cottage, poet William Wordsworth's homes. Hawkshead has a museum honoring Beatrix Potter and in Near Sawrey you can visit her home, Hill Top Farm, where she dreamed up such endearing characters as Mrs. Tiggy Winkle and the Flopsy Bunnies. *Directions:* Grey Friar Lodge is 1½ miles west of Ambleside on the A593, midway between Ambleside and Skelwith Bridge.

GREY FRIAR LODGE
Owners: Sheila & Tony Sutton
Clappersgate, Ambleside
Cumbria LA22 9NE, England
Tel & fax: (015394) 33158
E-mail: gflodge@aol.com
www.karenbrown.com/england/greyfriarlodge.html
8 rooms, 7 en suite
£24–£33 per person, dinner £16.50
Open Mar to Oct, Credit cards: none
Children over 12

Waterton Garden Cottage is part of a Victorian stable block that has been cleverly converted to two spacious homes. The house is set in a red-brick, walled garden of spacious lawns and flower beds with a heated swimming pool occupying a quiet corner beyond espaliered fruit trees. Ian, who has over 40 years experience in catering and hospitality, and his wife, Mary, work as a team preparing dinner, with Ian responsible for the main course and Mary concentrating on dessert. Guests are encouraged to bring their own wine to accompany the meal. What was once the tack room is now a paneled dining room hung with framed photographs of tempting food dishes. A narrow, spiral staircase leads up to the guests' bedrooms (larger suitcases are not a problem as Ian transports them via the main staircase). Bedrooms are prettily decorated and each is accompanied by a modern, en-suite shower room. If you care for tea or coffee, just ask and it will be served to you in the drawing room. Waterton Garden Cottage is a quiet countryside spot where a short drive will bring you to the heart of Cirencester. Southern Cotswold villages such as Bibury with its beautiful old cottages are within easy reach. *Directions:* From Cirencester take the A417 (Lechlade road) for 2½ miles to Ampney Crucis. Turn right before the Crown of Crucis Hotel, signposted Driffield. Take the first farm track to the right and Waterton Garden Cottage is at the end (do not pull into the courtyard).

WATERTON GARDEN COTTAGE
Owners: Mary & Ian Cassidy
Ampney Crucis
Gloucestershire GL7 5RX, England
Tel: (01285) 851303, Fax: none
3 en-suite rooms
£22.50–£30 per person, dinner £20
Open all year, Credit cards: none
Children over 9, No-smoking house

Whenever Elizabeth or Peter Hartland see people peering curiously up their driveway they know they're Richmonds looking for their roots, for Cove House was the home of John Richmond who went with the men of Taunton to found Taunton, Massachusetts, in 1640. The Richmonds belong to the Richmond Society, a group who can trace their ancestors back to this wisteria-festooned manor house. Guests enjoy breakfast in the gracious dining room where lovely flower arrangements dress antique furniture. In the small adjacent study, an alcove lined with a detailed map of the area illustrates the many places of interest round and about: Avebury, Blenheim Palace, Oxford, Bath, and the Cotswold villages. The bedrooms are large and some can take an extra child's bed and cot. Nearby, flooded gravel pits which attract many species of waterfowl provide a birdwatcher's paradise. Peter, a retired schoolmaster, keeps informational brochures on hand for visitors' use and has also compiled a "good food guide" to local pubs and restaurants. Guests often walk the short distance into the village to eat at the White Hart or the Horse and Jockey. With advance notice, Elizabeth is happy to prepare an evening meal for guests. *Directions:* The village of Ashton Keynes is 6 miles south of Cirencester. In the center of the village is the White Hart and 100 yards east a large wall bounds the driveway to Cove House. Drive through the inner gate.

COVE HOUSE
Owners: Elizabeth & Peter Hartland
2 Cove House
Ashton Keynes
Wiltshire SN6 6NS, England
Tel & fax: (01285) 861221
www.karenbrown.com/england/covehouse .html
3 en-suite rooms
£25–£28 per person, dinner £17.50
Closed Christmas, Credit cards: none
Children welcome, No-smoking house

The Barns is a comfortable spot to break a long journey between London and Edinburgh via the A1, or for a longer visit to explore Nottinghamshire. This county is famous not only for the exploits of Robin Hood, but also as the area where the Pilgrim Fathers formed their separatist church before setting sail for America and establishing a new colony. The Barns is the very tastefully converted hay and tractor barns of the next-door farm, and behind its red-brick façade all is spick and span. A sofa and chairs are drawn around a crackling log fire, and tables are topped with linen cloths neatly laid for breakfast. Upstairs, the bedrooms are plainly decorated with cream walls highlighting dark beams and all have nice touches such as a fresh posy of flowers on a small antique dresser and elegant china tea cups (one ground-floor room is also available). Rooms 1 and 5 are particularly large, more luxurious rooms. A pleasant drive through Sherwood Forest brings you to the visitors' center which has an exhibition on Robin Hood and his merry band and offers maps guiding you through ancient oak trees to his former hideaways. Clumber Park near Sherwood Forest is noted for its main driveway planted with over 1,296 lime trees. *Directions:* From the south take the A1 north to the A57 (Worksop) roundabout, make a U turn and go south on the A1. Take the first left, on the B6420, towards Retford. The Barns is on the left after two miles.

THE BARNS
Owner: Rosalie Brammer
Morton Farm
Babworth, Retford
Nottinghamshire DN22 8HA, England
Tel: (01777) 706336, Fax: (01777) 709773
www.karenbrown.com/england/thebarns .html
6 en-suite rooms
£21–£27.50 per person
Open all year, Credit cards: all major
Children welcome, No-smoking house

On a road of large, semi-detached Edwardian homes, Haydon House distinguishes itself as having the most colorful, pocket-sized garden. Magdalene has made the most of her home, decorating each of the rooms to perfection. Guests enjoy the sitting room with its plump sofas drawn cozily round the fire or the pocket-sized study with just enough room to spread your maps and books to plan the next day's adventures. The bedrooms are exceedingly pretty and named for the color of their decor: Strawberry, Gooseberry, Blueberry, Elderberry, and Mulberry. Request Blueberry or Elderberry if you want a more spacious room. Mulberry, tucked under the eaves, is an especially attractive triple or family room. With a choice of over 90 restaurants in the town, breakfast is the only meal served and includes a fresh-fruit platter and several other alternatives to a traditional, cooked English breakfast. Bath with its graceful, honey-colored buildings, interesting museums, and superb shopping merits several days' exploration. *Directions:* From Bath follow signs onto the A367 towards Exeter, pass an elongated roundabout by a railway viaduct, go up a hill to a small shopping area, and onto a dual carriageway (The Bear pub is on your right). At the end of the shops fork right into Bloomfield Road and take the second right (by the telephone kiosk) into Bloomfield Park.

HAYDON HOUSE
Owners: Magdalene & Gordon Ashman-Marr
9 Bloomfield Park
Bath
Somerset BA2 2BY, England
Tel & fax: (01225) 444919 & 427351
www.karenbrown.com/england/haydonhouse.html
5 en-suite rooms
£32.50–£37.50 per person
Open all year, Credit cards: all major
Children welcome, No-smoking house

Perched high above the city's rooftops, this large Victorian home offers every comfort to the visitor: luxurious bathrooms with heated towel rails and perfect showers, firm, American queen-sized beds, satellite television, in-house movies, picture-perfect decor, and the sincere attentions of George. Each of the bedrooms has its own flavor and, while I admired those in soft flowery pastels (the pink tower room with its lacy four-poster bed is very popular with honeymooners and there is a spacious ground-floor room for those who have difficulty with stairs), I particularly enjoyed the imaginative four-poster room where four turquoise obelisks are artfully draped in navy and white fabric to form the bedposts of this most interesting bed. Breakfast in the sunny green and yellow breakfast room offers lots of choices as well as the traditional English cooked breakfast. It's a 15-minute walk into town. George has designed driving tours with detailed instructions for a full day's sightseeing, so guests often venture as far afield as southern Wales. *Directions:* From Bath follows signs onto the A367 towards Exeter, pass an elongated roundabout by a railway viaduct, go up a hill, and take the first turning to the right into Upper Oldfield Park. Holly Lodge is the first house on the right just past the bend.

HOLLY LODGE
Owner: George Hall
8 Upper Oldfield Park
Bath
Somerset BA2 3JZ, England
Tel: (01225) 424042, Fax: (01225) 481138
www.karenbrown.com/england/hollylodge.html
7 en-suite rooms
£37.50–£42.50 per person
Open all year, Credit cards: all major
Children welcome, No-smoking house

Situated halfway up a steep hill, Somerset House is a classic Regency abode of warm, honey-colored stone, set in a spacious garden affording panoramic views of the city. The family pets (a parrot, dog, and cat), along with family photos and books give a comfortable feeling to the Seymours' upscale guesthouse. Decorated in pastels, the bedrooms have matching drapes and bedspreads and whimsical rag dolls propped up on the pillows. Several rooms have an extra bed and a ground-floor room is ideal for those who have difficulty with stairs. Bedrooms are named after the sons and daughters of George III and in their note to guests Jean and Malcolm have included the child's historical particulars as well as the rules of the house. Jean and Jonathan specialize in delicious regional English cuisine. Saturday nights (not in the summer) are particularly special, for Jean plans a theme meal (on the night of our stay it was France) and gives a verbal rendition of the menu, explaining the origins of the dishes and their tempting contents. The basement dining room complements the food, with light-wood Windsor chairs, lace-topped tables, and a huge pine dresser set upon the checkerboard tile floor. A 12-minute walk brings you into the heart of Bath. *Directions:* Do not go into the city center, but follow signs for the university. Going up Bathwick Hill, Somerset House is on the left.

SOMERSET HOUSE
Owners: Jean, Malcolm, & Jonathan Seymour
35 Bathwick Hill
Bath
Somerset BA2 6LD, England
Tel: (01225) 466451/463471, Fax: (01225) 317188
www.karenbrown.com/england/somersethouse.html
10 rooms, 9 en suite
£22–£32 per person, dinner £19
Open all year, Credit cards: all major
Children welcome, No-smoking house

Rosamund and John Napa were delighted to find this lovely Georgian House on a quiet street in the conservation village of Bathford just 3 miles from Bath. It was just what they had been looking for—a large home, suitable for bed and breakfast. Over the years they have added bathrooms and showers, decorated and slowly added antique furniture. It is by no means decorator perfect but the Napiers' warmth of welcome more than makes up for any decorational shortcomings. The spacious sitting room overlooks the grassy garden with its tennis court and guests help themselves to drinks at the honesty bar. Upstairs the larger bedrooms can be easily adapted to include an extra bed or two for children who stay here for a very reasonable rate. Each room is well equipped with color TV, phone, tea-making facilities, hairdryer, and en-suite shower or bathroom. If you would like complete privacy, opt to stay in one of the bedrooms in the walled garden cottage. Bathford is ideally situated for Bath and within easy reach of Bradford on Avon, Lacock, Longleat House, Stourhead Gardens, Bowood House, and Dyrham Park. *Directions:* From Bath take the A4 towards Chippenham for 3 miles, the A363 towards Bradford on Avon for 100 yards, then turn left up Bathford Hill. Church Street is the first right and Eagle House is on your right after 200 yards.

EAGLE HOUSE **New**
Owners: Rosamund & John Napier
Church Street
Bathford, nr Bath
Somerset BA1 7RS, England
Tel & fax: (01225) 859946
8 en-suite rooms
£28 per person
Closed Christmas, Credit cards: MC, VS
Children welcome

Frog Street Farm, a lovely gray-stone farmhouse dating back to 1436, is a real working farm where things are not fancy or cutesy pretty, but everything fits together perfectly with country freshness. From the moment you are met at the door by Veronica, with her true country-style warmth and jolly sense of humor, the mood is set. You are immediately made to feel part of the family and offered a cup of tea in front of the large inglenook fireplace before being shown to your room. The guestrooms are spotlessly clean and simply, but prettily decorated with a color scheme of pinks and greens used throughout. Behind the house lies the farmyard while to the front is a colorful garden and a swimming pool shaded by a tall hedge. Veronica takes great pride in her cooking and, with advance notice, will prepare delicious meals from farm-fresh produce. For those who want to spend a few days in the country, away from city sophistication, Frog Street Farm is the epitome of what a farm vacation should be. In this pretty, rolling countryside are the charming little towns of Chard, Ilchester, Ilminster, and Crewkerne. To the north the limestone Mendip Hills are honeycombed with spectacular caves and gorges such as Wookey Hole and Cheddar Gorge. The magnificent cathedral city of Wells is within easy driving distance. *Directions:* From the M5 take exit 25 and continue 4½ miles southeast to Hatch Beauchamp. Take Station Road to Frog Street Farm.

FROG STREET FARM
Owners: Veronica & Henry Cole
Beercrocombe
Taunton
Somerset TA3 6AF, England
Tel: (01823) 480430, Fax: none
www.karenbrown.com/england/frogstreetfarm.html
3 en-suite rooms
£25–£30 per person, dinner £16
Open Apr to Oct, Credit cards: none
Children over 11, No-smoking house

Set in a luxuriant garden, this 14th-century thatched Dartmoor longhouse, one of only a handful remaining, presents an idyllic picture. It has lots of charming features such as enormous granite fireplaces, sloping walls, low doors, exposed beams, and low, often sloping ceilings. Guests are welcomed with a traditional Devon cream tea and dinner is usually available on all but Saturday and Sunday evenings but must be ordered in advance (bring your own wine). The three small double bedrooms at the top of the steep, narrow staircase are cottage cozy, each with a double four-poster bed which hugs the ceiling. Two bedrooms have snug shower rooms in them while the third has its shower across the hall. Tor Down House is in Dartmoor National Park and a short walk up the lane finds you amidst the bracken and climbing up to the rugged tors. Gardens are popular with visitors and in the next village is one featuring the national collection of hostas. Rosemoor, the Royal Horticultural Society garden, is also nearby. *Directions:* Leave the A30 at the junction signposted Okehampton and Belstone (there are two Okehampton junctions). Follow signs for Belstone (2 miles) and in the center of the village take the lane that turns right immediately after the post office. You find Tor Down House's wooden five-bar gate after ¾ mile, soon after crossing the cattle grid.

TOR DOWN HOUSE
Owners: Maureen & John Pakenham
Belstone, Okehampton
Devon EX20 1QY, England
Tel: (01837) 840731, Fax: (01823) 480430
www.karenbrown.com/england/tordownhouse.html
3 rooms, 2 en suite
£27.50 per person, dinner £21
Closed Christmas & New Year, Credit cards:
MC, VS
Children over 14, No-smoking house
Wolsey Lodge

In the last century the owners of River Hall bought Biddenden's ancient market hall, moved it to their estate, and used it as a coach house. More recent occupants decided to incorporate the market hall into a traditional home. The sitting room was formerly the beamed market where farmers once sold their produce and upstairs the village meeting hall is the principal guest bedroom. An additional twin-bedded room—small only by comparison to its beamed neighbor—has a smart en-suite bathroom while the beamed bedroom's bathroom is large enough to accommodate both a bath and a separate shower. With advance notice, Sara is happy to provide a light supper or a three- or four-course dinner, whichever is required. The Sleighs are also glad to recommend restaurants and pubs round and about for dinner. In the morning guests make their way through the kitchen to enjoy breakfast in the conservatory which overlooks the sheltered garden. Within easy reach are the famous gardens of Sissinghurst and Great Dixter, the castles of Hever, Leeds, Scotney, and Bodiam, and the delightful cobbled streets of Rye. Farther afield lie Canterbury and Royal Tunbridge Wells. *Directions:* From Biddenden take the A262 towards Tenterden and take the first left-hand turn down a country road for about a mile to a T-junction. Turn left and River Hall Coach House is on your right.

RIVER HALL COACH HOUSE
Owners: Sara & Bill Sleigh
Biddenden
Kent TN27 8JE, England
Tel: (01580) 291565, Fax: (01580) 292137
www.karenbrown.com/england/riverhallcoachhouse.html
2 en-suite rooms
£26–£28 per person, dinner from £18
Open mid-Jan to mid-Dec, Credit cards: none
Children over 12, No-smoking house

This well-proportioned Victorian rectory is set in secluded grounds overlooking glorious vistas of the Derbyshire countryside. Geraldine and Stuart Worthington's solicitous welcome includes an invitation to the evening dinner party. Guests are introduced to each other over cocktails in the drawing room before sitting down at the large dining-room table, beautifully laid with silver and crystal. Geraldine and Stuart dine with their guests, Geraldine serving unobtrusively, with Stuart pouring the wine. After dinner, guests, host, and hostess return to the drawing room for port and coffee around the cheery log fire. The front bedroom has a large double bed framed by blue-and-white flowered draperies hung from a coronet, matching bedspread and bed ruffle, and an en-suite shower room. The large twin room has thick bathrobes so guests can pop comfortably across the hall to their bathroom. The third twin room tucked under the eaves has a steeply sloping ceiling and adjacent luxurious shower room. The dramatic and rugged Derbyshire scenery is a strong attraction for walkers. Many visitors also tour Chatsworth House, Haddon Hall, and the open-air Monday market in Bakewell. *Directions:* Leave Ashbourne on the A52 towards Leek. After 2 miles turn right towards Ilam. Drive through Okeover Park and turn left as you go through the gates. After 2 miles, at Blore crossroads, turn left and The Old Rectory is on your right beyond the church.

THE OLD RECTORY
Owners: Geraldine & Stuart Worthington
Blore, Ashbourne
Derbyshire DE6 2BS, England
Tel & fax: (01335) 350287
www.karenbrown.com/england/theoldrectory.html
3 rooms, 1 en suite
£38 per person, dinner £21.50
Closed Christmas, Credit cards: MC, VS
Children accepted over 15
Wolsey Lodge

Kath and Tony Peacock enjoy nothing more than singing with their church choir which is so noted for its musical prowess that it travels to Europe and America to give concerts. How appropriate with their ecclesiastical connection that they live in what was Boltongate's large, rambling, Victorian rectory. Tony loves to cook and stays busy in the kitchen while Kath has pre-dinner drinks with guests in the colorfully decorated drawing room. In contrast to the other tall-ceilinged, large-windowed rooms of the rectory, the dining room dates back to the 16th century and has a low beamed ceiling and a large inglenook fireplace with a wood-burning stove. Here guests dine together by lamplight, feasting on Tony's specialties. Bedrooms are large and comfortable, decorated with pretty wallpapers and matching drapes. Two have en-suite bathrooms while the largest has its bathroom (robes provided) down the hall. Boltongate is on the quiet, northernmost fringes of the Lake District, a perfect spot to break a journey to or from Scotland. Pretty towns and villages abound such as Caldbeck, Borrowdale, Ullswater, and Buttermere. William Wordsworth's birthplace is nearby in Cockermouth. *Directions:* Leave the M6 at exit 40, bypass Keswick and take the A591 for 7 miles. At the Castle Inn turn right at the sign for Ireby. Boltongate Old Rectory is the first house in the village on your right.

BOLTONGATE OLD RECTORY
Owners: Kathleen & Anthony Peacock
Boltongate
Cumbria CA5 1DA, England
Tel: (016973) 71647, Fax: (016973) 71798
www.karenbrown.com/england/boltongateoldrectory.html
3 rooms, 2 en suite
£35–£37 per person, dinner £23.50
Closed Christmas & New Year, Credit cards: MC, VS
Children over 14, No-smoking house
Wolsey Lodge

Visitors come to Pethills Bank Cottage to visit the sights in the region, then return because this bed and breakfast is the most delightful place to stay. Set high on a hill surrounded by fields, the cottage sits snug in an acre of rolling gardens overlooking the countryside. The cozy living room has thick, golden-stone walls and a large picture window framing the rolling lawn and rockery garden. The bedrooms are unexpectedly large, decorated in an unobtrusive, modern style which gives them a light, airy, and uncluttered feel. Each has an en-suite bathroom and a host of extras: biscuit jar brimming with tempting goodies, fruit bowl, mineral water, iron, hairdryer, remote-control television, shampoo, and bath oil. The Garden Room, decorated in pretty greens and creams, opens up to a verandah which overlooks the fields, The Dales Room also has magnificent countryside views and the largest bathroom. The Cottage Room has old-world charm with a beamed ceiling and low windows. The suite can be rented either on a bed-and-breakfast or self-catering basis. Breakfast fortifies you for the entire day as it includes an array of fruits, crisp bacon, sausage, eggs, tomatoes, mushrooms, and toast with homemade jam and marmalade. Yvonne helps guests plan visits to the Potteries factories and seconds shops (for example, Coalport, Royal Doulton, Minton, and Wedgwood). Derbyshire's dales and historic houses are close at hand. *Directions:* Bottomhouse is on the A523 between Leek and Ashbourne. Turn into the lane opposite the Little Chef restaurant and follow the signs up the hill for about a mile.

PETHILLS BANK COTTAGE
Owners: Yvonne & Richard Martin
Bottomhouse, Leek
Staffordshire ST13 7PF, England
Tel: (01538) 304277/304555, Fax: (01538) 304575
4 en-suite rooms
£21–£26 per person
Open Mar to mid-Dec, Credit cards: none
Children welcome, No-smoking house

This exquisite home takes its name from the Bourne Eau stream which runs alongside its grounds, separating it from an ancient abbey and a park. This house has evolved over the years and Dawn and George Bishop have decorated each room according to its historical period. The Elizabethan dining room has a flagstone floor topped with an Oriental carpet and a trestle table set before a huge inglenook fireplace beneath a low, beamed ceiling. The high-ceilinged, formal Georgian drawing room has enviable antiques and the snug Jacobean music room has a concert piano and a cheery log fire blazing in the ornately carved fireplace. Guests enjoy a scrumptious cooked breakfast in the low-ceilinged breakfast room furnished in mellow country pine. Bedrooms are equally lovely: the Jacobean Room with its period bed has a glorious modern bathroom; the large twin-bedded Georgian Room has a private staircase and views across the vast lawns; and the smaller twin-bedded room with private bathroom alongside overlooks the stream with its swans and ducks. Many guests visit Burghley House, Belton House, Belvoir Castle, and Stamford where the film *Middlemarch* was filmed. Many scenes in the T.V. production of *Moll Flanders* were filmed in Bourne in the Tudor Red Hall of Gunpowder Plot fame. *Directions:* Bourne is on the A15 between Peterborough and Sleaford. The house's concealed entrance is on the A15, 200 yards south of the town's main traffic lights, opposite the park.

BOURNE EAU HOUSE
Owners: Dawn & George Bishop
Bourne
Lincolnshire PE10 9LY, England
Tel: (01778) 423621 Fax: none
www.karenbrown.com/england/bourneeauhouse.html
3 en-suite rooms
£32.50–£35 per person, dinner £22.50 (wine included)
Closed Christmas & Easter, Credit cards: none
Children welcome by arrangement, Wolsey Lodge

Priory Steps, a row of 17th-century weavers' cottages high above the town of Bradford on Avon, is a glorious place to stay. The village tumbles down the hill to the banks of the River Avon, its narrow streets full of interesting shops and antique dealers. A few miles distant, the glories of Bath await exploration and are easily accessible by car or the local train service. Hostess Diana is a gourmet cook and guests dine *en famille* in the traditionally furnished dining room. While Diana's cooking is reason enough to spend several days here, the adjacent library with its books and pamphlets highlighting the many places to visit in the area provides additional justification. The bedrooms are all very different, each accented with antique furniture, and each has a smart modern bathroom, television, and tea and coffee tray. The Blue Room has large shuttered and curtained windows and a pleasing decor in shades of blue, while the large English Room has striped paper in muted tones of green coordinating with flowered curtains. There is a touch of whimsy in the bathroom of the dark-beamed Frog Room where an odd frog or two has inspired former guests to send their own contributions to an ever-growing collection of the creatures. The frogless bedroom itself is very pretty. *Directions:* Take the A363 from Bath to Bradford on Avon. As the road drops steeply into the town, Newtown is the first road to the right. Priory Steps is 150 yards on the left.

PRIORY STEPS
Owners: Diana & Carey Chapman
Newtown
Bradford on Avon
Wiltshire BA15 1NQ, England
Tel: (01225) 862230, Fax: (01225) 866248
www.karenbrown.com/england/priorysteps.html
5 en-suite rooms
£32–£34 per person, dinner £17
Open all year, Credit cards: MC, VS
Children over 12, Wolsey Lodge

After years of having a home both in England and Canada, Barbara and Barrie decided to settle in England and found the perfect house in this gracious Georgian home in Brampford Speke, a delightful little village just outside Exeter. Guests use the large drawing room which opens up to the large conservatory where Barbara serves breakfast. Upstairs are two very attractive bedrooms each accompanied by a dressing room and spacious bathroom. For those traveling with children an additional bedroom can be combined with one of the bedrooms to make a private family suite. For dinner, guests often walk to the nearby Agricultural Inn which serves good pub food as well as having an excellent restaurant, and Barbara has a list of recommended pubs and restaurants further afield. Jane Austen is supposed to have based her novel *Sense and Sensibility* hereabouts and Barbara will direct you to the nearby spots featured in the book. Further afield lies the north and south Devon coasts while closer at hand is Dartmoor with its villages nestled in green valleys with the moor high above. It's an ideal place to stay if you are attending the Exeter music festival which takes place for three weeks in July. *Directions:* From Exeter take the A377 towards Crediton. After passing over the Exe bridge on the outskirts of town turn right to Brampford Speke and Brampford House is on the left in the village, just beyond the church and before the red telephone box.

BRAMPFORD HOUSE **New**
Owners: Barbara & Barrie Smith
Brampford Speke, nr Exeter
Devon EX 5DW, England
Tel: (01392) 341195, Fax (01392) 841196
2 en-suite rooms
£35 per person
Open Mar to Oct, Credit cards: none
Children over 8

Gently rolling hills where sheep graze peacefully and shaded valleys with meandering streams surround the picturesque village of Broad Campden where The Malt House hugs the quiet main street and opens up to the rear to a beautiful garden. Years ago barley was made into malt here for brewing beer. Now a picturesque, country house, it provides a perfect central location for exploring other Cotswold villages. It is very much a family operation with Nick and Jean at the front of the house and son Julian as the talented chef. Julian offers three choices for each of the three dinner courses served in the inviting dining room where an open fire blazes on chilly evenings. Of the two lounges the little sitting room with its comfortable chairs arranged round the massive inglenook fireplace and mullioned windows offering glimpses of the garden is a favorite place to relax and toast your toes by the fire in winter. The bedroom décor ranges from cottage-cozy to contemporary, and all the immaculate bathrooms have old-fashioned tubs. Five bedrooms are in the house while an inviting ground-floor suite and two bedrooms are in the stable block. Lovely Cotswold villages to explore include Chipping Campden, Bourton-on-the-Water, Upper and Lower Slaughter, Stow-on-the-Wold, Bibury, and Broadway. Garden lovers will enjoy Kiftsgate, Hidcote Manor, and Batsford. *Directions:* On entering Chipping Campden, take the first right: you know you are in Broad Campden when you see the Bakers Arms. The Malt House is opposite the wall topped by a tall topiary hedge.

THE MALT HOUSE
Owners: Jean, Julian, & Nick Brown
Broad Campden, Chipping Campden
Gloucestershire GL55 6UU, England
Tel: (01386) 840295, Fax: (01386) 841334
www.karenbrown.com/england/themalthouse.html
8 en-suite rooms
£42.50–£44.50 per person, dinner £25.50
Closed Christmas, Credit cards: AX, VS
Children welcome

Just up the lane from The Malt House (our other Broad Campden listing) sits Orchard Hill House, the lovely mellow-stone farmhouse home of Caroline and David Ashmore and their two young children. Their low-beamed dining room sits at the center of the house and it is here that guests gather in the morning to enjoy breakfast round the long refectory-style table before the large inglenook fireplace. Upstairs are two delightfully decorated bedrooms, one with a snug en-suite shower room and the other with its private Victorian-style bathroom across the hall. While the rooms in the main farmhouse are very nice, I really enjoyed the privacy of going up the barn's stone staircase to the lofty, beamed Hayloft. Here you have a spacious room with a sitting area and twin and double beds. An adjacent twin-bedded room is set snugly beneath the barn's low beams. For dinner Caroline directs guests to the Bakers Arms in the village or makes suggestions from amongst the many excellent pubs, restaurants, and bistros in nearby Chipping Campden. Neighboring Snowshill is famous for its toy collection. The beautiful gardens of Kiftsgate and Hidcote are on the way to Stratford-upon-Avon which is just 10 miles away. *Directions:* On entering Chipping Campden take the first right. Pass the Bakers Arms pub and The Malt House, and Orchard Hill House is the next house on your left.

ORCHARD HILL HOUSE
Owners: Caroline & David Ashmore
Broad Campden
Chipping Campden
Gloucestershire GL55 6UU, England
Tel: (01386) 841473, Fax: (01386) 841030
www.karenbrown.com/england/orchardhilhouse.html
4 rooms, 3 en suite
£22.50–£28 per person
Closed Christmas, Credit cards: none
Children over 4, No-smoking house

Separated from the main road through Broadway by a grassy green, The Broadway Hotel dates back to Elizabethan times though it has had various additions over the years. The heart of the hotel is a tall, galleried sitting room whose white-plasterwork beamed walls rise to a raftered ceiling. The adjacent Jockey Bar with its horse-racing memorabilia is full of old-world pub atmosphere. Bedrooms stretch back in two wings with no two rooms being the same. I found the rooms that I saw to be of the plain and rather ordinary variety—more functional than luxurious, with fitted furniture. Four larger bedrooms (which I was unable to see) offer more space and Andrew tells me that they have more personality in their decor—well worth paying a few pounds extra for. Broadway is one of the most bustling Cotswold villages, along with Chipping Campden, Stow-on-the-Wold, and Moreton in Marsh. While you are in the area do not overlook the quieter, more off-the-beaten-path villages such as nearby Snowshill, where Snowshill Manor, a lovely Tudor home, is open to the public. *Directions:* Broadway is on the A44 between Evesham and Stow-on-the-Wold. The Broadway Hotel is almost directly opposite The Lygon Arms. A large car park is found at the rear.

THE BROADWAY HOTEL
Owner: Andrew Riley
The Green
Broadway
Worcestershire WR12 7AA, England
Tel: (01386) 852401, Fax: (01386) 853879
18 en-suite rooms
£40–£47.50 per person, dinner £17.95
Open all year, Credit cards: all major
Children welcome

Broadway with its attractive shops is one of the loveliest Cotswold villages and certainly one of the busiest. A stay at Milestone House not only gives you the opportunity to enjoy the village after the daytime crowds have left but also provides a convenient base for exploring this lovely part of the country. Like many of the houses in the village, Milestone House was built in the early part of the 17th century and is full of period charm. Guests have two comfortable sitting rooms and a large sunny conservatory where breakfast is served overlooking the garden. At dinner time guests choose from the array of eating establishments in Broadway and the surrounding villages. Up the narrow staircase you find three cottagey bedrooms. The two at the front of the house have shower rooms while a third enjoys a larger bathroom and overlooks the garden. Guests who are staying longer than a couple of nights particularly enjoy the courtyard room with its own private entrance. Doreen and Granville take lots of interest in their guests and encourage them to follow one of their driving itineraries through the off-the-beaten-track Cotswold villages. *Directions:* Broadway is off the A44 between Evesham and Stow-on-the-Wold. Milestone House is located on the High Street. There's a car park to the rear.

MILESTONE HOUSE
Owners: Doreen & Granville Shaw
122 High Street
Broadway
Worcestershire WR12 7AJ, England
Tel & fax: (01386) 853432
www.karenbrown.com/england/milestonehouse.html
4 en-suite rooms
£25 per person
Open all year, Credit cards: MC, VS
Children welcome, No-smoking house

In summer blowzy hollyhocks frame the door of College House, a substantial 17th-century home fronting a quiet street just off the village green of this peaceful Cotswold village. Old flagstones cover the floors, the walls have a soft pastel colorwash, and whimsical stenciling adds decorative interest to the shutters and the old fireplace which displays Sybil's collection of antique bottles. Nothing is cluttered or over-decorated. Sybil used to own a restaurant and is happy with advance notice to provide a three-course dinner. The main bedroom has a huge, luxurious bathroom decked out in blue and white; the bedroom is equally large, with a sleigh bed sitting center stage and an interesting priest hole with a small circular window and stencils of dwarf orange trees in tubs on the walls. Pale-lemon bows decorate the draperies and bed linen of The Yellow Room, blending beautifully with the soft-lemon-colored walls. The slipper tub in the bathroom is perfect for those who enjoy a deep soak and a read. The third bedroom is less expensive because its bathroom is up a spiraling wooden staircase in the attic. While guests visit Bath, Oxford, and Stratford-upon-Avon, Sybil finds what they enjoy most is following her tape that tours them through lesser-known Cotswold villages. *Directions:* From Stow-on-the-Wold take the A429 towards Moreton in Marsh. Turn right at the sign for Broadwell and Evenlode. College House is on your left on the Evenlode side of the village.

COLLEGE HOUSE
Owner: Sybil Gisby
Chapel Street
Broadwell, Moreton in Marsh
Gloucestershire GL56 0TW, England
Tel: (01451) 832351, Fax: none
www.karenbrown.com/england/collegehouse.html
3 rooms, 2 en suite
£23–£31 per person, dinner from £17.50
Open all year, Credit cards: none
Children over 16

The Buck Inn is a traditional Georgian coaching inn standing beneath the towering craggy heights of Buckden Pike which rises steeply behind it. Conviviality and good cheer are the order of the day in the bar where real ale is hand-pulled from the cool stone cellars. In summer there is always a crowd and overnight guests may prefer the quieter restaurant in a bright, enclosed courtyard where in days of old sheep auctions were held. You can enjoy a set four-course dinner with lots of choices for each course or order from the extensive bar menu. Bedrooms are country-style in their decor, the largest being a suite and four-poster room with a high, raftered ceiling. I particularly like those at the front with their view across the village to the dale. The surrounding rugged countryside offers many paths for walkers whether they prefer long day hikes or shorter strolls. Wharfedale has several lovely mellow-stone villages such as Grassington, Appletreewick, and Kettlewell. It is a spectacular drive from here through Coverdale to Middleham with its ruined castle and on to Jervaulx with its romantic ruined abbey. To the west, moorland roads lead to Arncliffe and Littondale and on to Malham (in Airedale), famous for its massive crags, tarn, and cove. *Directions:* Buckden is 18 miles north of Skipton on the B6160.

THE BUCK INN
Owners: Marjorie & Roy Hayton
Buckden
Skipton
Yorkshire, BD23 5JA, England
Tel: (01756) 760228, Fax: (01756) 760227
14 en-suite rooms
£31–£34 per person, dinner £14
Open all year, Credit cards: MC, VS
Children welcome

Deep in the Dorset countryside on the beautiful Isle of Purbeck, a farm track leads you to Bucknowle House which sits amongst rolling hills. The Victorians believed in spacious domestic architecture and as a consequence most of Bucknowle's rooms are large and all have high ceilings. Sara and Richard Harvey have papered the dining room in a pretty blue paper accented with gold stars and it is here that guests breakfast together around the large table. A family portrait of Sara, Richard, and their three sons hangs in the guest sitting room with its comfortable sofa and chairs drawn round the fireplace. Up the broad staircase the three homelike bedrooms are named after their color schemes: green, pink, and blue. All have attractive decor and fabrics that coordinate with the painted walls. All around you are quiet country lanes weaving through the Purbeck Hills to pretty villages. Interesting places to visit include the dramatic ruins of Corfe Castle, the sheltered bay of Lulworth Cove, the Arne Heath nature reserve, the old-fashioned resort of Swanage, the interesting town of Wareham whose roads were laid out by the Romans, Bournemouth, and the army tank museum at Bovington. *Directions:* From Wareham take the Swanage road (A351). Approaching Corfe Castle (4 miles), turn right immediately underneath the ruins, signposted to Church Knowle. A track on the left after half a mile is signposted for Bucknowle House.

BUCKNOWLE HOUSE
Owners: Sara & Richard Harvey
Bucknowle, Wareham
Dorset BH20 5PO, England
Tel: (01929) 480352, Fax: (01929) 481275
3 en-suite rooms
£20–£25 per person
Open all year, Credit cards: none
Children welcome

The clomp of hooves as horses pulled carriages down the main street of Burford has long disappeared, but the inns that provided lodging and food to weary travelers remain and if you are in search of a simple, quaint hostelry, you can do no better than to base yourself at The Lamb for the duration of your stay in the Cotswolds. A tall, upholstered settle sits before the fireplace on the flagstone floor of the main room, the hall table displays gleaming brass jelly molds, and an air of times long past pervades the place, particularly in winter when the air is heavy with the scent of wood smoke and a flickering fire burns in the grate. Narrow staircases and corridors zigzag up and down to the little bedrooms, all delightfully decorated in a charming cottagey style. In the dining room you make your choices from a three-course dinner menu. The homely little bar with its stone-flagged floor and wooden settles has an indefinable mixture of character and atmosphere. Burford's main street is bordered by numerous antique, gift, and tea shops. There are mellow-stone Cotswold villages to explore and Blenheim Palace and Oxford are less than an hour's drive away. *Directions:* Burford is midway between Oxford and Cheltenham (A40). The Lamb Inn is on Sheep Street, just off the village center.

THE LAMB INN
Owners: Caroline & Richard De Wolf
Sheep Street
Burford
Oxfordshire OX18 4LR, England
Tel: (01993) 840150, Fax: (01993) 822228
15 en-suite rooms
£45–£50 per person, dinner £24
Closed Christmas, Credit cards: MC, VS
Children welcome

Set amidst a row of grand Georgian townhouses fronting a broad square, Twelve Angel Hill is a delightful, upscale bed and breakfast operated with great professionalism by Bernadette (Bernie) and John Clarke. Breakfast is the only meal served in the formal dining room where little tables are topped with crisp linen cloths and surrounded by lovely antique chairs. In the evening guests often gather in the bar-cum-sitting room to discuss at which of the 40 nearby restaurants or pubs they are going to dine. Upstairs, the bedrooms range from enormous to snug and all but the four-poster room and the suite are priced the same. I especially enjoyed the two large front bedrooms with spacious seating areas (the four-poster room overlooks the back of the house). Light sleepers be aware there may be a little late-night noise from the square on Fridays and Saturdays. On the square you have the 16th-century cathedral and the church of St. Mary's (even older than the cathedral), and nearby two museums. If you are there on a Wednesday or Saturday, do not miss the street market. Bury St. Edmunds is an excellent center for touring East Anglia and Lavenham and Cambridge are popular places to visit. *Directions:* Follow the A14 to the Bury St. Edmunds ring road. Take the second exit (Bury St. Edmunds central) then at the next roundabout turn into Northgate Street. At the T-junction turn right into the square: Twelve Angel Hill is on your right (park at rear).

TWELVE ANGEL HILL
Owners: Bernadette (Bernie) & John Clarke
12 Angel Hill
Bury St. Edmunds
Suffolk IP33 1UZ, England
Tel: (01284) 704088, Fax: (01284) 725549
www.karenbrown.com/england/twelveangelhill.html
6 en-suite rooms
£35–£40 per person
Closed Jan, Credit cards: all major
Children over 16, No-smoking house

Pickett Howe is a picture-perfect, whitewashed farmhouse nestled amongst green fields beneath rugged Lakeland peaks. As you drive into the farmyard, Rowan, a golden retriever, greets you with enthusiastic tail-wagging and smiles. And, best of all, the interior lives up to all the promise of the exterior: there are polished slate floors topped with Oriental rugs, heavy oak beams, and small stone-mullioned windows set deep in thick stone walls. Sitting on the sofa chatting with Dani and David over tea and homemade cakes, you soon feel thoroughly at home. Upstairs, the four little bedrooms tucked neatly under the eaves have Victorian brass-and-wrought-iron beds, three have Jacuzzi bathtubs (and showers), while the fourth has a shower. Dani loves to cook and produces sumptuous dinners where there is always a choice of meat, fish, or vegetarian for the main course: small wonder that rigorous walking is often the order of the day. Dani and David were the 1997 national winners of the prestigious Booker Prize for Excellence in Bed and Breakfasts. Meander across Brackenthwaite Howe to sit quietly by Crummock Water or stride up Grasmoor. *Directions:* From exit 40 on the M6 take the A66 past Keswick, turn left onto the B5292 to Lorton, then follow signs for Buttermere. After 2 miles take the left fork (B5289) for Buttermere and the entrance to Pickett Howe is on your right after ¼ mile.

PICKETT HOWE
Owners: Dani & David Edwards
Buttermere Valley
Cumbria CA13 9UY, England
Tel: (01900) 85444, Fax: (01900) 85209
www.karenbrown.com/england/picketthowe.html
4 en-suite rooms
£37 per person, dinner £22
Open Mar to Nov, Credit cards: MC, VS
Children over 10, No-smoking house

Built over a century ago, Chilvester Hill House is a solidly constructed Victorian home isolated from the busy A4 by a large garden. Gill and John Dilley retired here and subsequently unretired themselves: John, a physician, now works as an occupational health consultant and Gill entertains guests and breeds beef cattle. Gill enjoys cooking and a typical (optional) dinner might consist of smoked trout, lamb noisettes with vegetables from the garden, fruit fool, and cheese and biscuits. They have a short wine list with over 20 French and German wines. A soft pastel decor, treasured antiques, and a cleverly displayed collection of commemorative plates make the large, high-ceilinged drawing room the most elegant room in the house. The bedrooms are spacious, high-ceilinged rooms, each individually decorated with flowery Sanderson wallpaper (two have zip-link beds that can be either a king or twins). All have mineral water, tea and coffee tray, television, tourist information, and private bathroom. Visitors can take advantage of Gill and John's maps marked with scenic routes to nearby Castle Combe, Lacock, and the Avebury Neolithic Circle. Bath, Oxford, and Salisbury are an easy drive away. *Directions:* From London leave the M4 at junction 14 and follow signs for Hungerford. Turn right on the A4 through Marlborough to Calne. Follow Chippenham signs for half a mile, turn right (Bremhill), and immediately right into the drive.

CHILVESTER HILL HOUSE
Owners: Gill & John Dilley
Calne
Wiltshire SN11 0LP, England
Tel: (01249) 813981, Fax: (01249) 814217
www.karenbrown.com/england/chilvesterhillhouse.html
3 en-suite rooms
£35–£42.50 per person, dinner from £18
Open all year, Credit cards: all major
Children over 12
Wolsey Lodge

Magnolia House, a sturdy Georgian home converted into the most welcoming of guest houses by Ann and John Davies, sits on a quiet street just a five-minute walk from the heart of Canterbury. Ann and John offer a sincerely warm welcome to their home and mark up maps of the city so that guests can easily find their way around. A small parlor is stacked with information not only on Canterbury but the surrounding area–you can easily keep busy for a week. Delightful guestrooms are found upstairs in the house ranging in size from a snug single to lovely double-bedded room, but the gem is the Garden Room with its private garden entrance, four-poster queen-sized bed, and the most spacious of bathrooms. In summer breakfast is the only meal served but on gloomy winter evenings Ann realizes that very often guests do not want to venture out and is happy, with prior arrangement, to provide supper. Canterbury is a lively historical city easily explored on foot. Its primary attraction is its cathedral, the Mother Church for all Anglicans. Begun in 1070, it has survived fires, wars, desecration, and bombing and became a pilgrimage site after the murder of Thomas à Becket. Join Chaucer's famous pilgrims in 20th-century re-enactment of the Canterbury Tales at the Canterbury Tales Museum in St. Margarets Street. *Directions:* Arriving in Canterbury on the A2 at the first roundabout turn left signposted University. St. Dunstan's Terrace is the third street on the right and Magnolia House is the first house on the left.

MAGNOLIA HOUSE   New
Owners: Ann & John Davies
36 St. Dunstan's Terrace
Canterbury CT2 8AX, England
Tel & fax: (01227) 765121
7 en-suite rooms
£32.50–£47.50 per person
Open all year, Credit cards: none
Children over 12, No-smoking house

Because of its quiet country location just 3 miles off the motorway, almost equidistant between Edinburgh and London, New Capernwray Farm is an ideal place to break a long, tiring journey. However, many weary travelers return for a proper country getaway to explore this unspoiled area. There really is nothing "new" about this solid, whitewashed stone farmhouse, for, despite its name, it is 300 years old. It was bought in 1974 by Sally and Peter Townend, who supervised its complete refurbishment while preserving its lovely old features, and now offer a very warm welcome to their guests. Before dinner you enjoy sherry in the cozy sitting room in front of a cheerful fire and then proceed to the dining room for a candlelit dinner. Bedrooms are particularly light, bright, and cheerful in their decor. The largest bedroom, with king bed, spans the breadth of the house, has a bathroom tucked neatly under the eaves and, as in all the rooms, is well equipped with tea, coffee, biscuits, television, hairdryer, mints, and a substantial sewing kit. A twin-bedded room has an en-suite shower room and the queen-bedded room has its shower room nearby. Sally and Peter offer guided tours and have a wealth of books and maps on the Lake District and the Yorkshire dales. *Directions:* Leave the M6 at junction 35 and from the roundabout follow signs for Over Kellet. Turn left at the T-junction into Over Kellet, then turn left at the village green: after 2 miles the farm is on the left.

NEW CAPERNWRAY FARM
Owners: Sally & Peter Townend
Capernwray
Carnforth
Lancashire LA6 1AD, England
Tel & fax: (01524) 734284
www.karenbrown.com/england/newcapernwrayfarm.html
3 rooms, 2 en suite
£29.50–£32 per person, dinner £19.50
Open all year, Credit cards: MC, VS
Children over 10, Wolsey Lodge

Carlisle makes an excellent place to break the journey when traveling by car between England and Scotland. Your host, Philip Parker, an ardent enthusiast of Carlisle and the surrounding area, encourages guests to use Number Thirty One as a base for visiting the city and exploring the northern Lake District and Hadrian's Wall. One of Philip's great passions is cooking and the dinner he prepares for guests depends on what is fresh in the market that day. Guests are welcome to bring their own wine to accompany the meal. Philip and Judith often join guests for a chat after dinner. Upstairs, the three bedrooms are equipped to a high standard, with TV, trouser press, tea tray, and hair dryer, and furnished in a style complementing this large Victorian terrace home. I admired the spaciousness of the Blue Room with its large bathroom and enjoyed the sunny decor of the smaller Green Room with its large dragon stenciled on the bedhead. The equally attractive Yellow Room has a half-tester bed and faces the front of the house. A ten-minute stroll finds you in the heart of Carlisle with its majestic cathedral and grand castle. Tullie House, an innovative museum, portrays Carlisle's place in the turbulent history of the Borders. *Directions:* Leave the M6 at junction 43 and follow Carlisle City Centre signs through five sets of traffic lights. Howard Place is the third turning on the right (before you reach the one-way system). Number 31 is at the end of the street on the left.

NUMBER THIRTY ONE
Owners: Judith & Philip Parker
31 Howard Place
Carlisle, Cumbria CA1 1HR, England
Tel & fax: (01228) 597080
www.karenbrown.com/england/numberthirtyone.html
3 en-suite rooms
£28–£38 per person, dinner £15
Open Mar to Nov, Credit cards: all major
Children over 16, No-smoking house

A country lane winds through Coverdale, one of the quieter Yorkshire dales, and leads to the few cottages and traditional dales pub, the Foresters Arms, that make up the village of Carlton. You enter into the snug low-ceilinged bar where you can enjoy ale on tap with the locals and warm yourself by the fire on cool evenings. The food is far more sophisticated than the run-of-the-mill pub grub and can be enjoyed in the bar or the little restaurant. Up the narrow stone staircase you find three small cottagey bedrooms and a quiet sitting area. Room 2 offers the most spacious accommodation (double bed) while room 1 (a twin) has a lovely view of the dale. Both have snug en-suite shower rooms. Room 3, a twin, has its private bathroom across the hall. Coverdale is a quieter, smaller dale that connects the busier Wharfedale to Wensleydale. Your hosts Julie Harrington and Barrie Higginbotham are happy to assist in planning walking and driving tours that encompass the stunning Yorkshire dales scenery and the characterful market towns. The ancient castles at Bolton, Skipton, and Middleham and the old abbeys of Jervaulx, Fountains, and Bolton are also worth a visit. *Directions:* Leave the A1 on the A6108 to Masham and on to Middleham. Proceed straight through the market square past the ruins of Middleham castle and into Coverdale. A 3-mile drive brings you to Carlton.

FORESTERS ARMS
Owners: Julie Harrington & Barrie Higginbotham
Carlton
Near Leyburn
Yorkshire DL8 4BB, England
Tel & fax: (01969) 640272
3 rooms, 2 en suite
£31 per person, dinner à la carte
Open all year, Credit cards: MC, VS
Children welcome

Theresa White, who hails from Edinburgh, prides herself on offering a warm Scottish welcome to her up-market bed-and-breakfast hotel located a brisk 20-minute walk from the heart of medieval Chester. When she bought Redland in the 1980s, it was very different from the flower-decked, frothily Victorian establishment you find today. Theresa has kept all the lovely woodwork and ornate plasterwork, adding modern bathrooms, central heating, vast quantities of sturdy Victorian furniture, four suits of armor, and masses of Victorian bric-a-brac. Guests help themselves to drinks at the honesty bar and relax in the sumptuous drawing room which includes among its array of furniture high-backed armchairs which almost surround you. Traditional Scottish porridge is a must when you order breakfast in the dining room where little tables are covered with starched Victorian tablecloths. For dinner Theresa is happy to advise on where to eat in town. Pay the few extra pounds and request one of the "best" rooms, for not only are they more spacious, but you will be treated to a lovely old bed (with modern mattress, of course) and decor where everything from the draperies to the china is color-coordinated. Walking round Chester's Roman walls is a good way to orient yourself to the city. It is fun to browse in The Rows, double-decker layers of shops. *Directions:* Redland Hotel is located on the A5104 1 mile from the city center.

REDLAND HOTEL
Owner: Theresa White
64 Hough Green
Chester CH4 8JY, England
Tel: (01244) 671024, Fax: (01244) 681309
www.karenbrown.com/england/redlandhotel.html
12 en-suite rooms
£27.50–£37.50 per person
Open all year, Credit cards: none
Children over 2

Chiddingfold, with its attractive homes set round the village green, is one of the most picturesque villages on the wooded Surrey Downs. A dovecote fronts the country lane just off the village green and a path leads beside it through a picture-book English cottage garden to Greenaway, the charming home of Sheila and John Marsh. The interior is just as delightful as the exterior, with low-ceilinged, beamed rooms, each decorated to perfection without making them stiffly formal or contrived. Guests enjoy the lovely living room with its views of the garden and part of Sheila and John's collection of colorful Staffordshire pottery displayed on the mantelshelf above the massive fireplace. Breakfast is served in the cozy dining room or, if guests prefer to sit and chat, they can eat their breakfast at the trestle table in the kitchen. For dinner guests often walk down to the 12th-century Crown Hotel in the village. The large front bedroom enjoys a new, old-fashioned bathroom with a claw-foot tub. The spacious blue twin and a third bedroom share a large immaculate bathroom. Chiddingfold is conveniently located 40 miles from both Gatwick and Heathrow airports. Guests often visit Petworth house, Bignor Roman villa, Chichester, Portsmouth, and the south coast. *Directions:* From Guildford take the A3 and the A283 to Chiddingfold. Pickhurst Road is off the green and Greenaway is the third house on the left with the large dovecote in front.

GREENAWAY
Owners: Sheila & John Marsh
Pickhurst Road, Chiddingfold
Surrey GU8 4TS, England
Tel: (01428) 682920, Fax: (01428) 685078
E-mail: jfrmarsh@niildwam.co.uk
www.karenbrown.com/england/greenaway.html
3 rooms, 1 en suite
£30–£35 per person
Open all year, Credit cards: none
Children welcome, No-smoking house

Ashen Clough, Isobel and Norman Salisbury's home, began life in the 16th century as a prosperous yeoman's home set in a rural Derbyshire valley. Norman was for many years the local vet then retired to take on domestic duties, helping Isobel run their lovely home as the most welcoming of Wolsey Lodges. Except on Sundays, guests dine with their hosts around the ancient refectory table in the low-beamed dining room. Drinks in the comfortable drawing room precede dinner and it is here that guests enjoy coffee and evening-long conversation before retiring to their delightful bedrooms. Country lanes lead to main roads that quickly transport you to Georgian Buxton with its restored opera house, Bakewell with its shops and Monday market, the Potteries where you can visit the Royal Crown Derby factories and factory shops, and the great houses of Chatsworth, Haddon, Keddleston, and Lyme Hall. *Directions:* From Buxton take the A6 (Manchester road) for 6 miles and at the roundabout turn left at the signpost for Chinley. Follow the B6062 into the village where you turn right and then right again into Maynestone Road. Ashen Clough is on your left after 1¼ miles.

ASHEN CLOUGH
Owners: Isobel & Norman Salisbury
Maynestone Road
Chinley, High Peak
Derbyshire SK23 6AH, England
Tel: (01663) 750311, Fax: none
www.karenbrown.com/england/ashenclough.html
3 rooms, 2 en suite
£28.50–£32 per person, dinner £19.50
Open all year, Credit cards: none
Children over 16, Wolsey Lodge

If you want to stay in a 600-year-old cottage at the heart of an idyllically pretty Cotswold town, you can do no better than Rosary Cottage, Rosemary Spencer's home in the center of Chipping Campden's High Street. However, be aware that this is one of the most popular Cotswold towns and parking in the daytime can be problematic. In the evening the tourists depart and the cottage-lined streets are yours to enjoy. Inside, Rosary Cottage is all exposed beams, low doorways, and sloping floors. Up the narrow stairs, the snug bedrooms are beautifully decorated and each has either a tiny en-suite shower room or its bathroom just outside the door—all are quite unsuitable for large suitcases. Rosemary encourages friendly conversation round the breakfast table and provides her guests with a bountiful repast—she used to be the breakfast cook at the Lords of the Manor hotel. Chipping Campden has an ancient market hall where sheep from the surrounding farms were sold, and there are lots of interesting little shops, two old churches, and a wide variety of restaurants, bistros, and pubs. A short distance away lies Hidcote, a series of alluring gardens each bordered by sculptured hedges and linked with paths and terraces. Next door, Kiftsgate has exquisite displays of roses. *Directions:* From Broadway take the A44, towards Stow on the Wold, up the hill and turn left for Chipping Campden. At the T-junction turn right into High Street and Rosary Cottage is on your left midway down the road.

ROSARY COTTAGE
Owner: Rosemary Spencer
High Street, Chipping Campden
Gloucestershire GL55 6AL, England
Tel: (01386) 841145, Fax: none
www.karenbrown.com/england/rosarycottage.html
3 rooms, 2 en suite
£22–£24 per person
Open all year, Credit cards: none
Children over 3

Oakfield is the elegant, early-Victorian home of Patricia and Peter Johnson-King, a home where standards surpass those of many country house hotels. Decorated in soft pinks and blue-grays, the enormous drawing room is warm and welcoming on even the dullest of days, its tall windows overlooking a broad sweep of lawns. Past the grand piano and up the elegant staircase are three lovely bedrooms. Elizabeth's Room has a half-tester bed softly draped in pale cream and turquoise with a huge claw-foot tub in the bathroom; Rose is a mass of pink and soft-blue cabbage roses; and Chinese is smartly Oriental with peach watered-silk wallpaper and a black satin bedspread coordinating with peach-and-black draperies. With advance notice, Patricia is happy to cook a four-course dinner which she and Peter share with their guests. Otherwise, guests often walk to Highwayman's Haunt. A full-size billiard room is there for you to use as is a large heated outdoor swimming pool. The gardens contain an unusual Victorian fern garden. Oakfield is ideally situated for exploring Dartmoor National Park, the cathedral city of Exeter, and the south Devon coast. *Directions:* From Exeter take the A38 towards Plymouth for 8 miles. Turn left for Chudleigh and after 1 mile Oakfield is on your right before you come to the center of the village.

OAKFIELD
Owners: Patricia & Peter Johnson-King
Chudleigh
Devon TQ13 0DD, England
Tel & fax: (01626) 852194
www.karenbrown.com/england/oakfield.html
3 en-suite rooms
£30–£35 per person, dinner £20
Open Easter to Oct, Credit cards: none
Children over 10, Wolsey Lodge

This pretty village of flint-walled, tile-roofed cottages is no longer "next the sea," but separated from it by a vast saltwater marsh formed as the sea retreated. The massive structure of Cley Mill stands as a handsome monument to man's ability to harness the forces of nature. Guests enter the mill directly into the beamed dining room decorated with country-style pine furniture. The circular sitting room has large chintz chairs drawn round a stone fireplace whose mantel is a sturdy beam displaying toby jugs. Stacked above the sitting room are two large circular bedrooms with en-suite bathrooms: the Wheat Chamber is where the grain was stored and the Stone Room is where the massive grinding stones crushed the flour. Two additional small bedrooms share a bathroom. During the day the mill is open to the public to visit the observation room and the wooden cap of the mill with its massive gears and complex mechanisms which once turned the grinding stones. The old boat house and stables in the yard have been converted into small, self-catering cottages. Birdwatching, sailing, cycling, and walking are popular pastimes in the area. The seaside towns of Sheringham, Cromer, and Wells are close at hand. There are a great many stately homes to explore such as Sandringham House, the Royal Family's country residence, Jacobean Fellbrigg Hall, Holkham, and Blickling Hall. *Directions:* From King's Lynn follow the A149 around the coast to Cley next the Sea, where the windmill is well signposted.

CLEY MILL GUEST HOUSE
Manager: Chris Buisseret
Cley next the Sea, Holt
Norfolk NR25 7NN, England
Tel & fax: (01263) 740209
www.karenbrown.com/england/cleymillguesthouse.html
7 rooms, 5 en suite
£27–£34.50 per person, dinner £16
Open all year, Credit cards: MC, VS
Children over 10

Sun Hill, a Yorkshire Dales farmhouse, is the loveliest of places to stay: a home that is furnished with enviable antiques, decorated in great style, and where Angela and Ian Close offer guests the warmest of hospitality and lovely food. The flagstone hallway leads to the conservatory where guests gather for pre-dinner drinks (drinks and wine are included in the tariff). Angela and Ian dine with their guests and join them afterwards in the sunny yellow sitting room with its comfortable Victorian chairs for coffee and conversation which often continues late into the night. Upstairs, the snug double bedroom has a spacious modern bathroom where Angela has painted a lovely frieze of wildflowers on the bathroom tile. The equally lovely twin-bedded room offers more space and has its large en-suite bathroom down a few stairs. Angela is an expert on antique shops and showrooms in the area—she has a good selection of bric-a-brac for sale in the adjacent barn and a stall at a local Sunday antique market. Sun Hill is ideally located for exploring the Yorkshire Dales, North York Moors, York, Castle Howard, and Fountains Abbey. Small wonder that guests return again and again. *Directions:* Exit the A1 at Bedale and turn right through the town towards Leyburn. Go through Crake Hall and Patrick Brompton to Constable Burton. Cross the bridge and turn first left. Follow the lane for 1 mile and Sun Hill is on your right near the top of the hill.

SUN HILL
Owners: Angela & Ian Close
Constable Burton, Leyburn
Yorkshire DL8 5RL, England
Tel: (01677) 450303, Fax: none
2 en-suite rooms
£35 per person, dinner £20
Open all year, Credit cards: none
Children welcome

Judy and Mike Ford confess to loving sailing, gardening, and Treviades Barton, their Cornish farmhouse which is above the River Helford and the Duchy Oyster Farm and opposite Frenchman's creek. While parts of the house date back to the 13th century, much of what you see today is the result of an extensive modernization in 1580. The ancient uneven flagstone floor leads you from the kitchen to the spacious low-ceilinged living room overlooking the walled garden. Follow the garden path from one flower-filled garden to another—this is where camellias bloom from January to June. With advance notice, Judy is happy to prepare dinner, which includes wine, and she and Mike usually join their guests. One of the bedrooms has an en-suite bathroom and little sitting area around the back of the chimney. If you are traveling with children, request the former children's rooms where two bedrooms share a bathroom. For a hassle-free excursion to the hidden villages and gardens of Cornwall, the Fords can put you in touch with James Agnew who specializes in personalized tours of this part of the country. *Directions:* From Truro take the A39 towards Falmouth. A small white sign indicates the turnoff to Constantine from the Hillhead roundabout on the A39 as it bypasses Penryn. Follow the signs for Constantine. Half a mile after High Cross garage turn left towards Port Navas and Treviades Barton is on your left (no name on the house).

TREVIADES BARTON
Owners: Judy & Mike Ford
High Cross
Constantine, near Falmouth
Cornwall TR11 5RG, England
Tel & fax: (01326) 340524
www.karenbrown.com/england/treviadesbarton.html
3 rooms, 2 en suite
£19–£25 per person, dinner £17
Closed Christmas, Credit cards: MC, VS
Children welcome

Nancemellan is a beautiful arts and crafts home overlooking the rugged little bay of Crackington Haven, built in 1905 for a wealthy Londoner. Lorraine and Eddie have taken great pains to keep all the lovely old features of the house with its tiled entryway, beams, and ornate door and window moldings. Guests have a lovely drawing room where a log fire is lit on chilly evenings. Breakfast is the only meal served round the large pine table in the family kitchen. Lorraine chats to guests about where to go and what to see as she cooks on the Aga. For dinner, guests can go just down the road to the pub or Lorraine is happy to make dining arrangements at local farmhouses that specialize in offering dinner for visitors. A large double bedroom offers the most glorious of sea views and has its spacious bathroom, resplendent with claw-foot tub, just across the hall. The other double-bedded room has its bathroom (also with claw-foot tub) en-suite while the twin-bedded room has its adjacent bathroom. Nine acres of gardens are yours to explore. The stunning views from the house tempt you out to the coastal path which offers the most magnificent of vistas of this rocky part of Cornwall. To the north lies Clovelly while to the south you find Boscastle and Tintagel. *Directions:* Ten miles south of Bude on the A39 turn right for Crackington Haven. As the lane begins to drop steeply towards the sea, Nancemellan is on your right.

NANCEMELLAN   New
Owners: Lorraine & Eddie Ruff
Crackington Haven, nr Bude
Cornwall EX23 0NN, England
Tel & fax: (01840) 230283
3 rooms, 1 en suite
£26–£30 per person
Closed Nov to Mar, Credit cards: none
Children over 16, No-smoking house

Just steps from the clifftops on a secluded stretch of Cornish coast, this 16th-century farmhouse snuggles in a hollow round a cobbled courtyard. The polished flagstone floors lead you into the comfortable sitting room with high-backed sofas grouped round the log-burning stove. Guests dine at separate tables and Janet Crocker offers a hearty dinner with a choice of starter, main course, and dessert. Farmhouse bedrooms range from small to spacious. If you are a party of four, opt for the roomier contemporary accommodation in nearby Samphire House. Here you enjoy two double bedrooms and a large sitting room with a balcony which overlooks a sheltered swimming pool. It's very much a family operation where Janet and her daughter Gayle run the farmhouse while her husband, four sons, and their wives manage the farm, tea room, and self-catering cottages. The farm is now licensed for civil marriages, offering a romantic spot to "tie the knot." The clifftops provide magnificent views and a path leads to Strangles Beach where Thomas Hardy loved to walk with his first wife Emma. Walking the coastal path and the nearby villages of Boscastle and Tintagel are great attractions. *Directions:* From Bude, take the A39 towards Camelford and then turn right to Crackington Haven. At the beach, take the right-hand turn at the bottom of the hill for Trevigue and you find Trevigue Farm atop the cliffs after 2 miles.

TREVIGUE FARM
Owners: Janet & Ken Crocker
Trevigue, nr Crackington Haven
Bude
Cornwall EX23 0LQ, England
Tel & fax: (01840) 230418
www.karenbrown.com/england/treviguefarm.html
5 en-suite rooms
£23–£28 per person, dinner £18
Open Mar to Oct, Credit cards: none
Children over 12

This idyllic picture-book farmhouse surrounded by a pretty garden and apple orchards is just a two-minute drive from the attractive town of Cranbrook with its white-board houses and shops, medieval church, and huge, white-board windmill with vast sails. Guests have a large sitting/dining room with comfy chairs set before an enormous inglenook fireplace and dine around a beautiful Georgian table, while separate tables are set for breakfast. The large downstairs bedroom has views to the garden and an en-suite shower room, and is large enough to accommodate an extra bed. Up a broad flight of creaking stairs is a glorious four-poster room where sunny yellow fabrics complement the dark woods of the floor and bed. The third bedroom has a small sitting room and en-suite bathroom and is prettily decorated with Laura Ashley fabrics. Sissinghurst Castle with its lovely garden is nearby and Bridget and Robin find that guests often visit Canterbury and its famous cathedral—they encourage them to time their visit to include choral evensong. The local vineyards and old railway at Tenterden are other popular attractions. *Directions:* Take the A21 south from Sevenoaks, turn left at the A262 before Lamberhurst, and right onto the A229. Go into Cranbrook and take a sharp left after the school. Tilsden Lane is the third right, and Hancocks' driveway the first track on the left.

HANCOCKS FARMHOUSE
Owners: Bridget & Robin Oaten
Tilsden Lane
Cranbrook
Kent TN17 3PH, England
Tel: (01580) 714645, Fax: (01580) 714645
www.karenbrown.com/england/hancocksfarmhouse.html
3 en-suite rooms
£28–£32.50 per person, dinner £20–£22.50
Open all year, Credit cards: none
Children over 9, No-smoking house

Everything about The Old Cloth Hall is exceptional, from the vast expanses of gardens with manicured lawns, roses, rhododendrons, and azaleas to the dignified old house, parts of which date back more than 500 years. Settle into the richly paneled drawing room with its commodious sofas and chairs drawn round the crackling log fire which blazes in the enormous inglenook. The Old Cloth Hall has been Katherine Morgan's home for many years and because it is a large house, she has an array of bedrooms that can be used for guest accommodation which she prices by size and location. If you want to splurge, ask for The Four-Poster room and you will receive a king-size four-poster decked and draped in lemon-and-green-sprigged fabric with an enormous bathroom. The small downstairs twin is reserved for children. Elizabeth I came for lunch in 1573 but you can stay for dinner and dine with your fellow guests. Guests are welcome to use the swimming pool and the tennis court. Cranbrook is one hour from London, Dover, Canterbury, and Brighton. Sir Winston Churchill's home, Chartwell, Knole, Igtham Mote, Penshurt Place, and Batemans, Rudyard Kipling's home, are within easy reach. *Directions:* Take the A21 south from Sevenoaks, turn left at the A262 before Lamberhurst and right onto the A229. Go into Cranbrook and take a sharp left after the school. Follow this road for about a mile, bearing left when it forks, turn right just before the cemetery, and the entrance to The Old Cloth Hall is on your right.

THE OLD CLOTH HALL
Owner: Katherine Morgan
Cranbrook
Kent TN17 3NR, England
Tel & fax: (01580) 712220
www.karenbrown.com/england/theoldclothhall.html
3 en-suite rooms
£42.50–£47.50 per person, dinner £20–£22
Closed Christmas, Credit cards: none
Children by arrangement, Wolsey Lodge

This quiet rural spot is just minutes from Scotch Corner on the A1, making it an ideal place to break your journey between the south of England and Scotland. David's family has always farmed in Yorkshire, and when he inherited this small farm, he moved here with Heather and built Clow Beck House. Heather and David are relaxed, welcoming people who truly enjoy sharing their home with visitors. Guests have a large formal drawing room but more often gravitate into the large country kitchen and the large beamed dining room with its cheery fire. A couple of rooms are in the main house with the remainder occupying a stable and granary wing. (One room in the granary wing is equipped for the handicapped.) All the rooms are excellently fitted with TV, phone, bathrobes, and large umbrellas. While breakfast is the only meal served, you can walk into the village for dinner and there are several other excellent places to eat within a few miles' drive. Use this welcoming, off-the-beaten-tourist-path spot as a base for explorations to the Yorkshire Dales, Moors, and heritage coast with Whitby, Robin Hood's Bay, and Runswick. Heather and David love planning routes for guests. *Directions:* From Scotch Corner go north on the A1 for a short distance to the Barton exit. Go through Barton and Newton Morell, turn right for Croft on Tees, and after 2½ miles turn left into the farm.

CLOW BECK HOUSE   ***New***
Owners: Heather & David Armstrong
Monk End Farm, Croft on Tees
Nr Darlington, Yorkshire DL2 2SW, England
Tel: (01325) 721075, Fax: (01325) 720419
E-mail: ifanet@cityscape.co.uk
11 en-suite rooms
£25 per person
Open all year, Credit cards: none
Children welcome

The Coach House is made up of a group of several old buildings, including a 1680s cottage and an old smithy, that form a square round a courtyard fronting directly on the A697 Coldstream to Morpeth road. The cottage serves as the dining room with two rooms either side of the entrance hall. Several of the nine bedrooms open directly onto the graveled courtyard—these are equipped for wheelchair access and each has a large open-plan bathroom. Most of the guestrooms have refrigerators and all have tea- and coffee-making facilities. A decadent afternoon tea of cakes and scones is laid in the high-beamed sitting room where French doors open onto the paved patio. Lynne offers an evening meal with a set main course and lots of choices of starters and dessert including several homemade ice creams. The decor is not perfect—a tad run-down in parts—but there's a lot of warmth and atmosphere to the place. Crookham makes an ideal place to break the journey between Scotland and York, but several days spent here will allow you to explore the plethora of Northumbrian castles and battlefields (Flodden is just down the road) and the delightful Northumbrian coastline between Lindisfarne (Holy Island) and the ancient port of Seahouses. *Directions:* From the south take the A1 to Morpeth and the A697 (Coldstream road) for 35 miles to Crookham where you find The Coach House on the left about a mile after the right-hand turn for Ford and Etal.

THE COACH HOUSE
Owner: Lynne Anderson
Crookham, Cornhill on Tweed
Northumberland TD12 4TD, England
Tel: (01890) 820293, Fax: (01890) 820284
www.karenbrown.com/england/thecoachhouse.html
9 rooms, 7 en suite
£23–£36 per person, dinner £16.50
Open Easter to Oct, Credit cards: none
Credit cards: MC, VS (4% extra)
Children welcome

When you stay at The Old Manor, you get far more than bed and breakfast in a 16th-century house—you can tour its motor museum, make friends with the army of ducks and geese that wander around the yard, and visit the contented, muddy pigs who wallow at the bottom of the garden. Inside there are cozy beamed rooms and the gentle ticking of Liz and John's clock collection. Books line the walls of the breakfast room and guests eat together round the trestle table before a log fire. The small yellow sitting room at the top of the stairs is for guests to use. A large double bedroom has a snug, en-suite shower room while the two twin rooms share a bathroom down the hallway. Liz is very aware that guests always enjoy their own bathroom facilities, so she rents only one of the twin bedrooms at a time. John is happy to show you his transportation collection which includes an AC Cobra, a 1910 AC Sociable, and a 1934 Aston Martin. If you are planning on staying for a week, consider renting the delightful little Dovehouse Barn. Warwick Castle, Coventry, and a multitude of Cotswold villages are within half an hour's drive. The Oxford Canal runs along the bottom of the garden and you can walk for miles along its towpath. *Directions:* Exit the M40 at junction 11 (Banbury) and take the A361 towards Daventry for 2½ miles, turn left to Cropredy, cross the canal, turn left at the T-junction, and The Old Manor is on your left.

THE OLD MANOR
Owners: Liz & John Atkins
Cropredy, Banbury
Oxfordshire OX17 1PS, England
Tel: (01295) 750235, Fax: (01295) 758479
E-mail: old_manor@cropredy.force9.net
www.karenbrown.com/england/theoldmanor.html
3 rooms, 1 en suite
£22–£25 per person
Closed Christmas & New Year, Credit cards: all major
Children welcome, No-smoking house

Fulford House is one of those fascinating homes that has evolved over the years. The earliest parts date back to the 1600s with various bits added from time to time—hence the interesting way you step up and down as you go from room to room. Guests are welcomed as visiting friends and encouraged to make themselves at home in the comfortable sitting room with its slipcovered chairs and soft-peach walls. Blowzy roses decorate the curtains and bed ruffles of the largest bedroom whose en-suite bathroom is up a short flight of stairs. A large twin room and a small single sharing a bathroom across the hall are suitable for families. A booklet in each bedroom gives an in-depth history of Culworth and suggests enough sightseeing excursions to keep you busy for a week, including Sulgrave Manor, George Washington's ancestral home, Warwick Castle, Stratford-upon-Avon, Coventry Cathedral, exquisite Hidcote Manor gardens, and Fulford House's own acre of delightful gardens which Marypen and Stephen are justifiably very proud of. *Directions:* From the M40 junction 11 roundabout take the A422 towards Brackley, then after 1 mile take B4525 signposted Northampton. After 2 miles turn left to Culworth. Turn right alongside the village green and Fulford House is on your left.

FULFORD HOUSE
Owners: Marypen & Stephen Wills
Culworth
Banbury
Oxfordshire OX17 2BB, England
Tel: (01295) 760355, Fax: (01295) 768304
3 rooms, 1 en suite
£24–£30 per person, dinner £17.50*
*parties of 6 only
Open all year, Credit cards: none
Children over 5

The Cott Inn is the longest thatched building in Devon and certainly one of the prettiest pubs in England with its little windows peeking out coyly from beneath the thatch and the garden a blaze of color. On entering, you see a comfortable bar with low, beamed ceiling, horse brasses, log fire, and locals drinking pints of bitter. A wide selection of dinner specials is posted on the blackboard or you can choose from the short steak menu. If you prefer to eat in more sophisticated surroundings, choose the little dining room where a tempting array of desserts is laid out on the buffet. Up the narrow winding staircases the cozy bedrooms tucked under the thatch come in attractive doubles or twins and are accompanied by en-suite bathrooms or shower rooms. Just down the road is Dartington's Cider Press shopping center where in amongst the craft shops you find the Dartington Glass Shop. Nearby Totnes has its castle and streets of ancient buildings: on Tuesdays in summer the townsfolk dress in Elizabethan costume. Farther afield lie Elizabethan Dartmouth with its naval college, picturesque Salcombe, Buckfastleigh with its abbey, and the wild expanses of Dartmoor National Park. *Directions:* Travel on the A38 towards Plymouth when the M5 ends and turn left on the A384 towards Totnes. As you enter Dartington, pass a church on your left and at the next roundabout take the second exit to Cott. Cott Inn is on your right after half a mile.

COTT INN
Owners: Susan & David Grey
Cott, Dartington
Devon TQ9 6HE, England
Tel: (01803) 863777, Fax: (01803) 866629
6 en-suite rooms
£27.50–£30 per person, dinner £10–£17.50
Open all year, Credit cards: all major
Children over 5

Ford House is a three-story, Regency-style home which was built for the owner of one of the many shipyards that flourished in Dartmouth during the 19th century. It is now owned by laid-back Australian Dick Turner. Guests go upstairs and downstairs to their bedrooms from the combination sitting and dining room. Garden-level bedrooms are confusingly called the King Room (it has an American queen-sized bed) and the Twin Room, which, more often than not, has its twin beds zipped together as a king. Upstairs you find Tony's Room, where old sewing machines decorate the top of the armoire and the bed is placed at an angle to capture the view across the rooftops of the town. While there are lots of restaurants in town, Dick is happy, with advance notice, to provide an evening meal if guests do not want to go out again after a long day's sightseeing. A fun day trip involves taking a ferry and steam train into Paignton. On Tuesdays in summer you can take the ferry to Totnes and stroll around the market admiring the townsfolk in their colorful Elizabethan costumes. *Directions:* From Totnes, take the A381 to Halwell and the A3122 to Dartmouth, where you take the first feeder lane to the right into Townstal Road, which becomes Victoria Road. If you go down a long straight hill, you've gone too far.

FORD HOUSE
Owner: Dick Turner
44 Victoria Road
Dartmouth
Devon TQ6 9DX, England
Tel & fax: (01803) 834047
3 en-suite rooms
£25–£50 per person, dinner £25
Open Mar 14 to Oct, Credit cards: all major
Children welcome

Delbury Hall, built in 1753, is one of the most beautiful Georgian houses in Shropshire, a grand red brick edifice reflected in a lake with elegant swans. Despite its gracious architecture and lovely antiques, this is not an intimidating or overly grand house, but very much a home for Lucinda and Patrick Wrigley and their two young children. You enter directly into the imposing two-story entry hall with its staircase sweeping up to the gallery above. Here you find a four-poster room with a large en-suite bathroom and a suite of rooms with two bedrooms and a bathroom, which is often used for families. A spacious twin-bedded room has its private bathroom up a further flight of stairs. Guests help themselves to drinks at the honesty bar while Patrick prepares an elegant dinner with fruits and vegetables fresh from the garden. The lake includes a trout fishery where guests can try their hand at catching rainbow trout. Medieval Ludlow with its spectacular ruined castle and plethora of interesting antique shops is a ten-minute drive away. Other attractions include the Ironbridge Gorge museums and the Severn Valley Steam Railway. *Directions:* From Ludlow take the A49 north towards Shrewsbury and take the first right (B5365) signed Much Wenlock for 5 miles. Turn right on the B4368 to Diddlebury then right before the village at The Lodge for Delbury Hall. If you miss this turn, go into the village and follow signs for Delbury Trout Fishery.

*DELBURY HALL   **New***
Owners: Patrick & Lucinda Wrigley
Diddlebury, nr Craven Arms
Shropshire SY7 9DH, England
Tel: (01584) 841267, Fax: (01584) 841441
E-Mail: wrigley@delbury.demon.co.uk
4 rooms, 1 en suite
£40–£45
Closed Christmas, Credit cards: none
Children welcome

Hunts Tor offers the opportunity not only for very comfortable bed and breakfast accommodation but also for enjoying excellent food (Paul Henderson of Gidleigh Park assured me that, next to Gidleigh Park, Sue Harrison offers the finest food on Dartmoor). Every evening Sue prepares a set, four-course dinner and while she is busy in the kitchen husband Chris helps guests choose wine and serves at table. In 1997 Hunts Tor was nominated by the Good Food Guide as the "Best Small Devon Restaurant of the Year." Fortunately for diners, the Harrisons also offer the highest quality accommodation (Gidleigh Park excluded, of course!) in the area. The three very spacious bedrooms are large enough to accommodate seating areas. The raw beauty of Dartmoor with its sheltered villages and market towns, wild ponies, and spectacular scenery is a magnet for walkers and those touring by car. Just beyond the village you find Castle Drogo, the castle-like house designed by Lutyens. *Directions:* Take the M5 to Exeter and the A30 towards Okehampton for about 14 miles. Turn left for Drewsteignton (3 miles) and upon reaching the village square turn right. Hunts Tor is at the opposite end of the square from the church.

HUNTS TOR
Owners: Sue & Chris Harrison
Drewsteignton
Devon EX6 6QW, England
Tel: (01647) 281228, Fax: none
www.karenbrown.com/england/huntstor.html
3 en-suite rooms
£30–£35 per person, dinner £20–£23
Open Mar to Oct, Credit cards: none
Children over 10

Dunster, with its adorable main street dominated by the battlements and towers of Dunster Castle, is a picture-postcard village. Dollons House, once a pharmacy whose chemist also made marmalade for the Houses of Parliament, is a gift shop of English crafts and silk flowers where proprietor Humphrey Bradshaw makes his marmalade for his family and bed and breakfast guests. Up the narrow cottage stairs guests have a cozy sitting room which leads to a patio and pocket-sized garden. Hannah Bradshaw has taken a great deal of care decorating her very pretty bedrooms. Teddy, as the name implies, has cute bears embroidered on its towels and pillows and a whimsical honey-bear mural decorating the tiny shower room. Tulips is soft and country in pale pinks with hand-painted tulips on the fabric border which edges the room. Kate's at the back of the house is delightfully white and frilly with a large bathroom and shower. Dunster Castle is open to the public and you can tour the 18th-century Dunster watermill. *Directions:* From Bridgwater take the A39 almost to Minehead. Turn left on the A396 into Dunster, and Dollons is in Church Street on your right. Pull up outside to unload then park in the High Street or behind the church.

DOLLONS HOUSE
Owners: Hannah & Humphrey Bradshaw
Church Street
Dunster
Minehead
Somerset TA24 6SH, England
www.karenbrown.com/england/dollonshouse.html
Tel: (01643) 821880, Fax: none
3 en-suite rooms
£25–£27 per person
Closed Christmas, Credit cards: MC, VS
Children over 15, No-smoking house

Drakestone House is an exceptional Cotswold-style home filled with an abundance of lovely antiques. The well kept grounds invite a leisurely stroll between the tall, clipped hedges laid out by Hugh's grandfather. The interior of Drakestone House has lovely old pine-pitch-and-jarrah wood floors and beamed-and-plasterwork ceilings, complemented by traditional firebaskets filled with dried-flower arrangements and beautiful old furniture. Guests enjoy breakfast round the dining-room table where Crystal will, with advance arrangements, also serve dinner for guests' first evening's stay. Upstairs, two bedrooms share the facilities of an old-fashioned bathroom which has been modernized. There is also a suite which has an adjoining private bathroom, a small single room suitable for children (crib available), and/or a larger, twin-bedded room which has windows with views both to the side and the front of the house. From Drakestone House you can visit Berkeley Castle and the adjacent Jenner Museum, Slimbridge Wildfowl Trust, Westonbirt Arboretum, and, farther afield, Gloucester, Cheltenham, Bath, and Bristol. *Directions:* Northbound travelers leave the M5 at exit 14; southbound at exit 13. Stinchcombe is situated halfway between Dursley and Wotton-under-Edge on the B4060. Drakestone House is signposted on the road.

DRAKESTONE HOUSE
Owners: Crystal & Hugh St. John Mildmay
Stinchcombe
Dursley
Gloucestershire GL11 6AS, England
Tel: (01453) 542140, Fax: none
www.karenbrown.com/england/drakestonehouse.html
3 rooms, none en suite
£25 per person, dinner £17.50
Open Mar to Oct, Credit cards: none
Children welcome, No-smoking house
Wolsey Lodge

Ronald's acres of garden have been voted among the top three in Somerset: plant-filled borders line the tumbling stream, the herbaceous border is ablaze with summer flowers, and the water meadow offers some unusual plant species. Jackie loves to share her beautiful home with guests who can choose from three very different bedrooms. The Cottage Suite offers a low-ceilinged bedroom, snug sitting room with television and sofas which can be made into extra beds, and a small bathroom. In contrast, the Master Suite offers a large high-ceilinged room with a queen-sized bed, television, and a large, luxurious Victorian-style bathroom. The Pine Bedroom takes its name from the enormous pine fitted cupboard that has been there since the house was built. You are welcome to bring your own wine to accompany dinner. If you prefer to eat out, try the Foresters Arms, just a two-minute walk away. There are ten classic gardens in South Somerset. Wells and Glastonbury are within easy touring distance, as is the Dorset Coast. *Directions:* From Yeovil, take the A30 (Crewkerne road) for 2 miles to the Yeovil Court Hotel. Turn immediately left at the signpost for North Coker, and Hardington. Pass the Foresters Arms, and Holywell House is the next driveway on the right. (Ignore all signposts for East Coker.)

HOLYWELL HOUSE
Owners: Jackie & Ronald Somerville
Holywell
East Coker
Yeovil
Somerset BA22 9NQ, England
Tel: (01935) 862612, Fax: (01935) 863035
www.karenbrown.com/england/holywellhouse.html
3 en-suite rooms
£30–£32.50 per person, dinner £17
Closed Christmas & New Year, Credit cards: none
Children welcome

Anthony's forbears have farmed hereabouts for over 300 years and he continues in the family tradition. When Alison and Anthony married, they knocked two small cottages into one and added on to the rear to form a spacious home with gardens terracing down to fields and the most spectacular view across the sky-wide fens to Ely Cathedral, a building so large that it dwarfs the little market town that surrounds it. This captivating vista is enjoyed by a very spacious guest bedroom which occupies a wing at the end of the house. At night the cathedral is floodlit and presents a spectacular sight. The bedroom is light and fresh, with white walls, flowered drapes, pretty bedspread, and immaculate en-suite shower room. Breakfast is the only meal served round the table in the delightful conservatory and guests often dine at The Anchor in Sutton Gault or The Fire Engine House in Ely which serves traditional Fenland food such as smoked eel and pheasant. Cambridge, whose university complex spans over 700 years of history, is a big draw for visitors who stroll through its college courtyards, explore its ancient alleys, and punt or row under the willow trees that line the River Cam. Among Ely's narrow streets are the house where Cromwell lived, Goldsmith's tower and museum, and the enormous cathedral built in 1083. *Directions:* Take the A10 from Cambridge to Ely, approximately 14 miles, turn right at the roundabout onto the A142 towards Newmarket, and Stuntney is on your right. Lower Road is opposite the church.

FORGE COTTAGE
Owners: Alison & Anthony Morbey
Lower Road, Stuntney, Ely
Cambridgeshire CB7 5TN, England
Tel & fax: (01353) 663275
www.karenbrown.com/england/forgecottage.html
1 en-suite room
£30–£32.50 per person
Closed Christmas, Credit cards: none
Children over 6, No-smoking house

Over 500 years ago this tiny cottage in this quiet Cotswold village was home to the parish priest and today is a welcoming bed and breakfast. The front door opens into the large guest sitting room where a lovely Welsh dresser holds an array of unusual green-and-white china and the breakfast room whose massive inglenook fireplace is decorated with country knickknacks. An old lamp hangs over a large round table where guests gather for breakfast which consists of their choice of traditional bacon and eggs or smoked haddock and kippers. The free-range eggs come from the farm next door and honey from Jan's bees. The three guest bedrooms found at the top of the narrow stairs have lots of simple country charm and each has its own bathroom. A double room has old pine furniture while the large twin has roses peeking in at the window and a view across the fields. Above the stable a one-bedroom self-contained flat is available for bed and breakfast or self catering. Husband David, a banker mason, has carved new stone-mullioned windows for the cottage. Exploring the Cotswolds with their rolling hills and pretty villages is most enjoyable, but guests also love shopping for clothes and antiques, and visiting gardens such as those at Kiftsgate and Hidcote. *Directions:* Take the Cotswold villages of Chipping Norton, Stow-on-the-Wold, and Moreton in Marsh as a triangle on the map and the small village of Evenlode is at the center of the triangle.

TWOSTONES
Owners: Jan & David Wright
Evenlode
nr Moreton in Marsh
Gloucestershire GL56 0NY, England
Tel: (01608) 651104, Fax: none
www.karenbrown.com/england/twostones.html
3 rooms, 2 en suite
£20 per person
Open all year, Credit cards: none
Children over 10, No-smoking house

It was love at first sight when I rounded the bend in the driveway and saw this beautiful Elizabethan manor house. As I drove up Tosca, a golden retriever greeted me with enthusiastic tail-wagging and Fiona came out to meet me. Best of all, the interior lived up to all the promise of the exterior: there's a Tudor staircase, extensive Elizabethan paneling, and magnificent mullioned windows. The rose garden fills the entire drawing room window and sitting on the sofa enjoying a convivial pre-dinner drink with Fiona and Peter, who also dine with their guests, you soon feel thoroughly at home. Upstairs are three lovely bedrooms of a standard you find in the most luxurious of country house hotels. The house is large enough that the Wilcoxes have one wing and guests have the other. Wells with its gorgeous cathedral and Glastonbury steeped in Arthurian legend are popular places to visit. Interesting houses nearby include Hestercombe, designed by Lutyens with a Jekyll garden, Montacute where "Sense and Sensibility" was filmed, and Barrington Court with its cabinetmakers and lovely garden. *Directions:* Leave the M5 at junction 25 and take the A358, then the A378 towards Langport to Fivehead. Turn right just before the garage, left at the bottom of the hill, and go straight (not round the bend)– Langford Manor is on your left after 300 yards.

LANGFORD MANOR **New**
Owners: Fiona & Peter Wilcox
Fivehead, nr Taunton
Somerset TA3 6PH, England
Tel: (01460) 281674, Fax: (01460) 281585
3 en-suite rooms
£35 per person, dinner £20
Closed Christmas, Credit cards: none
Children over 14, No-smoking house

Hyde Farm House was once the principal farm on the Frampton estate. When the estate was sold, Frampton Manor was transported stone by stone to America and the farmhouse fell upon sad times, being rescued by John and Jan who took five years to restore it to the glorious home you see today. The minimum of regimentation is the order of the day, so guests can dine at the time of their choosing and while John cooks, Jan (he hails from Norway) looks after guests, seating them either at the long table in the dining room or in the conservatory overlooking the garden. Guests are encouraged to bring their own wine. Strains of classical music accompany dinner and coffee in the most inviting of drawing rooms. Staffordshire flatback figures (Napoleon, Dick Whittington, and Queen Victoria amongst them) line the staircase which leads to the delightful bedrooms. Chatsworth is a particularly elegant room with its draped bed and large bathroom. This rural corner of Dorset is Thomas Hardy country, set between Maiden Newton (Chalk Newton) and Frampton (Scrimpton) and just 7 miles from the sea at Abbotsbury. It is an easy drive to over 20 gardens and 15 National Trust properties. Bring your rod and enjoy Hyde Farm House's private fishing. *Directions:* Take the A37 from Dorchester towards Yeovil for 5 miles and turn left on the A356 (Crewkerne road) into Frampton. Pass the church on your right, the village hall your left, and Hyde Farm House is on your left after 500 yards.

HYDE FARM HOUSE
Owners: John Saunders & Jan Faye-Schjoll
Dorchester Road
Frampton, nr Dorchester
Dorset DT2 9NG, England
Tel: (01300) 320272, Fax: none
3 en-suite rooms
£27.50 per person, dinner £15
Open all year, Credit cards: none
Children over 13, No-smoking house

When Mary and Tony Dakin bought The Old Parsonage at an auction, it was in a sad state of disrepair and they have put a great deal of work into making it the lovely home you see today. In the days when clerics were men of substance, there were six servants for the house and garden, but now it's just Mary, Tony, their two sons, and the tractor-mower. In the morning, Tony cooks breakfast while Mary assists guests. Typical of grand Georgian houses, the rooms are tall and spacious and the Dakins have furnished them in a most delightful manner. Two of the bedrooms have double-bedded four-posters while the third is a spacious twin-bedded room. One of the four-poster rooms has a shower room while the other two rooms have bathrooms with large tubs and separate showers. Tony is a keen gardener—the sunny conservatory is always full of plants—and photographer—photos of longtime village residents line the hallway and historic Frant pictures, together with Mary's tapestries of village scenes, adorn the dining room. Frant is a most attractive village set round a green, with two pubs and a restaurant where guests usually go for dinner. Information folders in the bedrooms give details on the 15 houses, castles, and gardens to visit in the area. London is a 40-minute train ride from Frant station. *Directions:* From Tunbridge Wells, take the A267 south for 2½ miles to Frant. Turn left at the 30 mph Frant sign, and The Old Parsonage is on your left, just before the church.

THE OLD PARSONAGE
Owners: Mary & Tony Dakin
Church Lane, Frant, Tunbridge Wells
Kent TN3 9DX, England
Tel & fax: (01892) 750773
www.karenbrown.com/england/theoldparsonage.html
3 en-suite rooms
£30–£33.50 per person
Open all year, Credit cards: MC, VS
Children welcome

The soothing sound of water splashing down the mill race is the only sound that breaks the countryside peace and quiet when you stay at Maplehurst Mill, the site of a mill since 1309. Heather feels that eating here is an integral part of the stay and guests dine by candlelight in the ancient miller's house with its beams and inglenook fireplace. Bottomend, a ground-floor bedroom, sits directly above the mill race and its windows open onto the moss-covered millwheel. Topend, at the top of the mill, has a beamed bathroom and the four-poster room which overlooks the meadows has its bed strategically placed on the sloping floor. The room across the garden in the stables lacks the warm country character of those in the mill. A heated swimming pool overlooks the fields. Idencroft Herb Gardens are just round the corner and Brattle Farm, an old-fashioned working farm, is an excellent choice for those who have visited all Kent's castles, gardens, and stately homes. *Directions:* From the M20 take the A229 Hastings exit and follow Hastings signs through Maidstone for 12 miles to Staplehurst. At the end of the village turn left into the Frittenden road. After 1¼ miles, opposite a white house, turn right into a narrow lane. At the end turn right and the mill is at the foot of the incline.

MAPLEHURST MILL
Owners: Heather & Kenneth Parker
Mill Lane
Frittenden
Kent TN17 2DT, England
Tel & fax: (01580) 852203
www.karenbrown.com/england/maplehurstmill.html
5 en-suite rooms
£29–£35 per person, dinner £19
Open all year, Credit cards: MC, VS
Children over 12, No-smoking house
Wolsey Lodge

With its acres of lovely gardens, grass tennis court, and heated swimming pool, Ennys is an idyllic, 17th-century manor house set deep in the Cornish countryside, 3 miles from St. Michael's Mount. Polished flagstones line the hallway leading to the garden where on fine summer evenings guests gather at 7 o'clock for a chat over sherry before going in to dinner at four little tables set around the fireplace. On cool evenings, drinks are served in the cheery sitting room. Upstairs are three lovely bedrooms, two of them delectable four-posters. Families are welcome in the suites which occupy an adjacent barn—bedrooms here are also delightfully appointed, though without the bric-a-brac that children find so hazardous. St. Michael's Mount is a "must do," as is spending an evening at the open-air Minack Theater in Porthcurno. A delightful day trip involves an hour's countryside walk (or a short drive) to the railway station where you take a train to St. Ives to visit the Tate Gallery which displays the work of 20th-century St. Ives artists. *Directions:* From Exeter, take the A30 to Crowlas village which is 4 miles before Penzance. Turn towards Helston, at the roundabout, and at the next roundabout turn left at the signpost for Relubbus. Go through Goldsithney to St. Hilary, and when the Ennys Farm's signpost is on the right, turn left and follow the lane for a mile to the farm.

ENNYS FARM
Owners: Susan & John White
St. Hilary, Goldsithney
Penzance
Cornwall TR20 9BZ, England
Tel & fax: (01736) 740262
www.karenbrown.com/england/ennysfarm.html
5 en-suite rooms
£22.50–£30 per person, dinner from £17.50
Closed Christmas, Credit cards: MC, VS
Children over 2 welcome in family suites

Ashfield House sits on a quiet little courtyard just off Grassington's main street. I loved this 17th-century house from the moment I stepped through the low doorway into the quaint little parlor where an old polished settle sits beside a massive log-burning fireplace. Another little sitting room has groupings of chairs and an honesty bar where guests enjoy a pre-dinner drink before going into the little cottagey dining room. Keith offers a set four-course dinner with choices of starters and dessert. In the winter and spring when guests return earlier from sightseeing and walking, Linda and Keith offer scones and tea at 4:30 pm and then a three-course dinner at 7 pm. The bedrooms open up beyond their low doors and some are quite spacious. Two have lovely views of the garden while one has a close-up view of the adjacent cottage but the advantage of a larger bathroom. All bedrooms have compact shower rooms, TVs, and tea-making facilities. To experience some magnificent scenery, take a breathtaking circular drive from Grassington and back again through Littondale, over the fells to Malham Cove, and back to the village. *Directions:* From Skipton take the B6265 to Grassington. Turn into the main street, pass the cobbled square, and turn sharp left after the Devonshire Hotel onto a cobbled access road which leads to Ashfield House.

ASHFIELD HOUSE
Owners: Linda & Keith Harrison
Grassington
Skipton
Yorkshire BD23 5AE, England
Tel & fax: (01756) 752584
7 en-suite rooms
£26–£38 per person, dinner £13.50–£17
Open Feb to Christmas, Credit cards: MC, VS
Children over 5, No-smoking house

Sitting beside the village green at the heart of this quiet, unspoilt Cotswold village, The Lamb is a picture-perfect hostelry. Locals gather in the evening in the quaint bar where pride of place is given to a picture gallery of guide dogs for the blind who have been sponsored by patrons' donations. Decked out in pine, the restaurant with its soft-pink decor is most attractive. The menu is à la carte with such dishes as beef Wellington and grilled lamb cutlets with onion sauce. Simpler fare is served in the bar and adjacent buttery. Up the narrow, winding staircase and down twisting, narrow corridors are an array of cottage-style bedrooms, all furnished differently (suitable only for the nimble of foot). Two have intricately carved four-poster beds made by Richard. Thick stone walls with deeply set windows, low ceilings, quaint doors, and beams all add to the old-world feel. Two new attractive garden suites with terraces and king-sized beds, Jemima's House and Millie's House, are very popular choices. The two rooms in the converted stable are not as attractive. Outside is a landscaped garden—the perfect place to enjoy a glass of real ale on a warm summer evening. Most people come here to tour the picturesque Cotswold villages, explore gardens such as Hidcote, and visit Stratford-upon-Avon and Oxford. *Directions:* From the A429 turn into Bourton-on-the-Water, carry on along this road (not into the village), and take the first turn right to Great Rissington.

THE LAMB INN
Owners: Kate & Richard Cleverly
Great Rissington
Bourton-on-the-Water
Gloucestershire GL54 2LD, England
Tel: (01451) 820388, Fax: (01451) 820724
www.karenbrown.com/england/thelambinn.html
14 en-suite rooms
£22.50–£42.50 per person, dinner £14–£18
Open all year, Credit cards: all major
Children welcome

Church House, a spacious Georgian home, has a sweep of driveway circling to the front door beneath massive copper beeches. To the rear are lawns, sheep pasture, and a helicopter landing pad for those who care to arrive by air. Guests have a high-ceilinged comfortable yellow drawing room where Anna displays her collection of paintings by West-Country artist Reg Gammon. Anna is happy, with advance notice, to prepare dinner. Guests eat together round the long polished table and you are welcome to bring your own wines. A graceful wooden staircase spirals its way up to the top floor and the homey guestrooms. The largest bedroom has its private bathroom across the hall while the other three rooms have their facilities in the room, artfully concealed behind tall wooden screens. Ask for the one with the view from the loo of Grittleton rooftops. On the landing is an information table showing all the things to do and see in the area, though guests are welcome to spend their days relaxing around the heated swimming pool. Grittleton is well placed to visit Bath, Bristol, Malmesbury, Tetbury, and the picture-perfect village of Castle Combe. Every May the Badminton horse trials are held nearby. *Directions:* Exit the M4 at junction 17, taking the A429 towards Cirencester, and almost immediately (at the crossroads) turn left for the 3½-mile drive to Grittleton. Church House is beside the church.

CHURCH HOUSE
Owners: Anna & Michael Moore
Grittleton, Chippenham
Wiltshire SN14 6AP, England
Tel: (01249) 782562, Fax: (01249) 782546
www.karenbrown.com/england/churchhouse.html
4 rooms, 3 en suite
£27.75 per person, dinner £16
Open all year, Credit cards: none
Children under 2 & over 12

Surrounded by a sky-wide landscape of fields, this converted 19th-century oast offers spacious accommodation within a half hour's drive of Kent's most celebrated tourist attractions. The lower half of the roundels, where the hops were roasted, has been converted into a spacious sitting room, but, more often than not, guests gather in the open-plan kitchen which was formerly a barn. Anne is happy to provide dinner with advance notice. Two bedrooms (a twin and a double) occupy the upper reaches of the roundels and share a well-equipped bathroom. The third bedroom is very large and has its bathroom en suite. Sasha, the friendly golden retriever, is a great favorite with guests. Anne gives her guests lists of places to visit and a map of pubs and restaurants in the area to assist them in making sightseeing and dining decisions. Nearby places of interest include Chartwell (Churchill's home), 13th-century Hever Castle, the onetime home of the Boleyn family, and Penshurst Place, a 14th-century manor house. *Directions:* From Tonbridge, take the A26 towards Maidstone. After the village of Hadlow, pass Leavers Manor Hotel on the right and turn right into Stanford Lane. Leavers Oast is the third driveway on your right.

LEAVERS OAST
Owners: Anne & Denis Turner
Stanford Lane
Hadlow
Kent TN11 0JN, England
Tel & fax: (01732) 850924
www.karenbrown.com/england/leaversoast.html
3 rooms, 1 en suite
£26–£29 per person, dinner £18
Open all year, Credit cards: none
Children over 12, No-smoking house

There are many good reasons to visit Leicestershire and this exceptional home at the edge of a peaceful village with many picturesque thatched cottages is one of them. Here old furniture is gleamingly polished, the windows sparkle, and everything is in apple-pie order. The evening sun streams into the drawing room where books on stately homes and castles invite browsing. Breakfast is served in a small dining room with a long trestle table. If there are several people for dinner, Raili (who grew up in Finland) sets the elegant table in the large dining room and serves a variety of meals using organic vegetables from her garden. The principal bedroom has en-suite facilities, while the other guestrooms have either private bathrooms or shower rooms. Bedrooms have televisions and someone is always on hand to make a pot of tea. A three-day Christmas program gives guests the opportunity to experience a quiet, traditional English country Christmas—visits to the hunt and the midnight carol service are highlights. Nearby are a great many stately homes (Burghley House and Rockingham Castle, for instance), lots of antique shops, cathedrals at Ely and Peterborough, historic towns (Stamford and Uppingham), and ancient villages. *Directions:* From Uppingham take the A47 and turn left at East Norton for Hallaton. Drive through the village and The Old Rectory is next to the church.

THE OLD RECTORY
Owners: Raili & Tom Fraser
Hallaton
Market Harborough
Leicestershire LE16 8TY, England
Tel: (01858) 555350, Fax: none
3 rooms, 1 en suite
£28 per person, dinner £16
Open all year, Credit cards: none
Children over 7, No-smoking house
Wolsey Lodge

Sandbarn Farm was originally part of the Lucy family's estate at nearby Charlecote. During the 1980s this 16th-century farmhouse was extensively modernized and now it is home to Helen and Paul Waterworth who offer guests a quiet countryside retreat just ten minutes' drive from Stratford-upon-Avon. Guests have a snug television lounge and eat breakfast together round the dining-room table. A pub in the village serves meals, but Helen is also happy to suggest restaurants in Stratford. Under the eaves, two large bedrooms can either be twin-bedded or have their beds zipped together as kings, and each has a spacious bathroom and additional single bedroom (no reduction for children). A third bedroom has its private bathroom across the hallway. The Lucy family have resided across the fields at Charlecote Park since 1204 in a gracious home which was modernized during the 19th century. You can tour the Victorian kitchens and grand rooms and enjoy beautiful walks through vast acres of parkland. While Stratford-upon-Avon is a must to visit, also remember to wander into Warwick, with its mixture of Georgian and old timber houses and magnificent castle. *Directions:* Exit the M40 at junction 15, and take the A46, Stratford road. At the next roundabout, fork left on the A439 signposted Stratford Town Centre. Turn left at a small crossroads (with a large Mercedes showroom) to Hampton Lucy, and Sandbarn Farm is on the right after 1½ miles.

SANDBARN FARM
Owners: Helen & Paul Waterworth
Hampton Lucy
Warwickshire CV35 8AU, England
Tel: (01789) 842280, Fax: none
www.karenbrown.com/england/sandbarnfarm.html
3 en-suite rooms
£25 per person
Closed Christmas, Credit cards: none
Children over 5

Surrounded by lush green fields, Greenlooms Cottage offers a quiet countryside location just 5 miles from the heart of medieval Chester. The cottage was the hedger-and-ditcher's cottage on the Duke of Westminster's Eaton estate. Hezekiah, the last incumbent, lived here for many years with his sister Miriam who raised pigs and geese. Now Greenlooms is home to Deborah and Peter Newman who have sympathetically extended and modernized the cottage, while keeping all its lovely old features such as the low, beamed ceilings and the pump in the garden. Step through the front door into the old-fashioned pine country kitchen where Deborah serves breakfast. Through the snug television room you come to the cottagey little bedrooms. For dinner, Deborah usually suggests the Grosvenor Arms in Aldford or dining in the atmospheric bar at nearby Willington Hall. Rather than looking for parking in the center of Chester, drive to the Park and Ride from where a shuttle bus transports you into town (runs every ten minutes till 6 pm). Conwy Castle and Bodnant Gardens in Wales are a very popular day trip. *Directions:* From Chester take the A41 (Whitchurch road) south for 2 miles, and turn left at Whitehouse Antiques (before the Black Dog pub). Follow the road through the village for 1½ miles, turn right into Martins Lane, and Greenlooms Cottage is on your right, after less than a mile.

GREENLOOMS COTTAGE
Owners: Deborah & Peter Newman
Hargrave
Chester
Cheshire CH3 7RY, England
Tel: (01829) 781475, Fax: none
2 en-suite rooms
£20–£25 per person, dinner £10
Open all year, Credit cards: none
Children welcome, No-smoking house

Christine and David Cooper have lovingly converted this mill, barn, and mill house (mentioned in the Domesday Book of 1086) into a secluded hideaway set amid woodland, water, and pasture. Steep stairs, nooks, crannies, and low doors and ceilings are all part of the fun and character of staying here. In the mill the Dutch-door entrance leads into a sitting room with two round grinding stones on the floor and antique pulleys and gears above. From here separate steep, narrow staircases lead up to two delightful snug bedrooms (small suitcases only). Although compact, each bedroom is bright and cheery with sun streaming in from the overhead skylight. The bathrooms are reached by ladder-like steps down from the bedrooms (definitely not a place to stay for the infirm). The adjacent old wooden barn is all beams and coziness. Downstairs there are a sitting room and bedroom and up the stairs rustic doors lead to two additional bedrooms. The romantic four-poster room's bed is made partially from the timbers of a haywagon. In the double bedroom you duck beneath a beam to enter the bathroom. Breakfast is served in the Coopers' mill house. A light supper tray can be ordered. *Directions:* Take the A264 from Tunbridge Wells, then go 1 mile south on the B2026 towards Hartfield. Turn left just past Perryhill Nurseries on the farm track and keep right at the Y.

BOLEBROKE MILL
Owners: Christine & David Cooper
Edenbridge Road
Hartfield
Sussex TN7 4JP, England
Tel & fax: (01892) 770425
www.karenbrown.com/england/bolebrokemill.html
5 en-suite rooms
£28.50–£37 per person
Closed Christmas & Jan, Credit cards: all major
Children over 7, No-smoking house

The mill wheel still turns today as it has, with a short hiatus, since 870 when the Saxons built a wooden mill on this sight. The millstream burbles through the acres of lovely garden which is open to the public, as is a small section of the mill which serves teas and lunches. To enjoy the mill in its entirety, stay overnight with Eva and Martin and dine with them at the table before the huge inglenook fireplace. The guests' sitting room enjoys a log fire, cable TV, CD player, and French windows opening up to a balcony overlooking the gently turning millwheel. Off the sitting room are two absolutely lovely guestrooms, one with an en-suite bathroom and the other with a shower. Follow the tumbling River Speke down the valley to see it cascade 60 feet onto the beach and then stroll along the cliffs to Hartland Quay. More serious walkers head south along the coastal path to Welcome, returning in time for dinner. Just up the road you can tour Hartland Abbey, a home dating to 1157, and walk through its rather neglected gardens down to a private beach. A short drive brings you to Clovelly, while farther afield lie the very attractive seaside towns of Lynton and Lynmouth. *Directions:* From Bideford take the A39 south towards Bude and then follow signs for Hartland. At this junction you see a brown sign for Docton Mill–follow the flowers to the mill: turn left in Stoke and follow signs for Elmscott which is just beyond the mill.

DOCTON MILL   New
Owners: Eva & Martin Bourcier
Spekes Valley, Hartland
Devon EX39 6EA, England
Tel & fax: (01237) 441369
2 en-suite rooms
£38.50 per person, dinner £21.50
Closed Christmas & New Year, Credit cards: MC, VS
Children over 14, No-smoking house

It was love at first sight when I came upon Carr Head Farm sitting high above Hathersage village with steep crags and windswept heather moors as a backdrop. The garden presents a large flagstone patio, a profusion of flowers nestled in little niches in the terraces leading down to a sweeping lawn, and the most spectacular view across this beautiful Derbyshire valley. The beauty of Mary Bailey's gardens is matched by the loveliness of her home where everything has been done with caring and impeccable taste. The beamed dining room is furnished in period style with groupings of tables and chairs where guests gather for breakfast, the only meal served. The adjacent drawing room is very elegant in blues and creams, a bowl of sweets sitting on the coffee table next to a stack of interesting books. The two lovely bedrooms have en-suite facilities. The four-poster room offers beautiful views of the valley. The Peak District with its picturesque villages, stone-walled fields, and dramatic dales is on your doorstep, as are Haddon Hall and Chatsworth House. *Directions:* Exit the M1 at junction 29 towards Baslow where you take the A623 to the B6001, through Grindleford to Hathersage. At the junction with the main road, turn right up the village, left into School Lane, and first left. Just before the church (Little John of Robin Hood fame has his grave in the churchyard) turn right up Church Bank to the farm.

CARR HEAD FARM
Owners: Mary & Michael Bailey
Church Bank, Hathersage
Hope Valley S32 1BR, England
Tel: (01433) 650383, Fax: (01433) 651441
E-mail: michael.bailey@tyzack.com
www.karenbrown.com/england/carrheadfarm.html
2 en-suite rooms
£24–£26 per person
Closed Christmas, Credit cards: none
Children over 12, No-smoking house

Hawnby is a quiet little village in the heart of the North York Moors with a few houses, a shop, a Wesleyan chapel, and a drovers' inn. In 1996 Colin and Barbara Archbell purchased a long-term lease on The Hawnby Hotel, a small, simple, country hotel with a lively public bar, giving the hotel the warmth of owner management. Barbara looks after and cooks for guests while Colin assists and tends the bar. Their long-term project is to restore the bar to its former traditional feel while offering guests a warm welcome. Sofas and chairs are grouped round the fire at one end of the sitting room and at the other end little tables are set for dinner or breakfast. Dinner is good home cooking with choices in each of the three courses, but I did not like the glass-topped tables and paper napkins. The decor throughout is soft and pretty, with flowery drapes, attractive bedspreads, and pretty wallpapers. The bedrooms are named after their predominant color, with Cowslip pretty in soft yellows, Jade a favorite with jade-green wallpaper, and Rose a smaller room of soft pinks with roses. Rooms are designated either smoking or no-smoking. Apart from walking, guests love visiting and exploring the traditional Yorkshire villages with their open-air markets. *Directions:* Helmsley is on the A170 midway between Thirsk and Pickering. Turn along the side of the marketplace and follow B1257 signposted Stokesley out onto the moor. Hawnby is signposted to your left after 3 miles. Note that guests are not able to check in between 3 and 6 pm.

THE HAWNBY HOTEL
Owners: Barbara & Colin Archbell
Hawnby near Helmsley
N. Yorks Y06 5QS, England
Tel: (01439) 798202, Fax: (01439) 798344
6 en-suite rooms
£25–£27.50 per person, dinner £12.50
Open Mar to mid-Jan, Credit cards: MC, VS
Children welcome

Sheltered in a gentle fold of the hills beneath the spectacular crags of Haytor Rocks, Haytor Vale is a quiet village containing little cottages and The Rock Inn. With its wooden beams and huge open fireplace, the inn has a cozy, traditional ambiance. Bedrooms are named after horses that have won the Grand National: Lovely has an old oak four-poster bed and a dark-beamed ceiling, Master Robert and Freebooter are rooms with sloping ceilings and large private bathrooms. A relatively small supplement is charged for these deluxe rooms, and it is well worth paying. All the bedrooms have television (including a movie channel), tea and coffee, telephone, and a mini-bar. The food here is delightful: bar meals range from traditional roasts to curries (the desserts are especially tempting), while the candlelit restaurant serves a set-price dinner with a wide variety of choices for each course. From the giant rocky outcrop of neighboring Haytor Rocks you can see the vast extent of Dartmoor National Park, the Teign estuary, and the rolling hills of southern Devon. The nearby quarry supplied the stone used for building London Bridge, which now resides in America. *Directions:* Take the M5 from Exeter which joins the A38, Plymouth road, then the A382 to Bovey Tracey. At the first roundabout turn left and follow the road up to Haytor and cross a cattle grid onto the moor. After passing an old gas station, turn left into Haytor Vale.

THE ROCK INN
Owner: Christopher Graves
Haytor Vale
Newton Abbot
Devon TQ13 9XP, England
Tel: (01364) 661305, Fax: (01364) 661242
E-mail: rockin@eclipse.co.uk
9 rooms, 8 en suite
£29.95–£45.50 per person, dinner à la carte
Open all year, Credit cards: AX, VS
Children welcome

Jane Harman is an enthusiastic gardener and loves to host fellow enthusiasts who come to tour the many lovely gardens in Kent. Guests have their own entry which leads to a charmingly furnished low-beamed dining room with its brick floor and walls lined with interesting books. Guests dine together round the polished table by the soft glow of candlelight. In the adjacent sitting room gleaming copper and brass accent the huge 16th-century inglenook fireplace, usually lit for guests on chilly evenings. Upstairs, creaking, crooked floors lead to the bedrooms and I particularly admired the spacious Blue Room. The Middle Room's bathroom is next door to it, but plans are afoot to break through the walls, so it may be en suite by the time you visit. Downstairs is a spacious twin room while across the courtyard additional bedrooms (or self-catering accommodation) are found in the cottage. Jane has a folder on places of interest to visit (you'll need to stay a month if you plan on visiting them all!). Another folder covers gardens, amongst the more famous of which are Sissinghurst, Doddington, Mount Ephraim, Goodnestone, and Great Dixter. You can make day trips to London. *Directions:* Exit the M20 at junction 8 towards Leeds Castle. Go through Leeds village to the A274, turn left and go through Sutton Valence and 1 mile beyond Headcorn to the crossroads. Turn right signposted Waterman Quarter and Vine Farm is on the left after ¾ mile.

VINE FARM
Owners: Jane & Tim Harman
Waterman Quarter, Headcorn
Kent TN27 9JJ, England
Tel: (01622) 890203, Fax: (01622) 891819
3 en-suite rooms
£23–£27.50 per person, dinner £18
Closed Christmas, Credit cards: MC, VS
Children over 12, No-smoking house

Helm is a scattering of farmhouses sitting high on the open hillside offering magnificent views of Wensleydale. On the far right of this group of houses you find the 17th-century farmhouse also called Helm—John and Barbara's home. A colony of doves in the ornamental dovecote adds to the charm of the place. A tiny entrance hall brings you into the stone-flagged dining room with its beamed ceiling (there are over 30 choices of wine with dinner). At the bottom of the little staircase you find a massive stone cheese press used in the farmhouse for the production of Wensleydale cheese. Two delightful bedrooms, a twin and a double, facing the front of the house have panoramic dales views and compact shower rooms. A third bedroom, a very snug and cozy double room, faces the rear of the house and has a larger bathroom with a Victorian tub. The nearby Kings Arms pub has an old-fashioned bar that appeared as the Drovers Arms in the James Herriot television series. A short walk over the fields brings you to the dramatic waterfalls of Whitfield Gill and Mill Gill. Farther afield lies the village of Hawes where you can visit the Wensleydale Creamery to watch cheese being produced. *Directions:* Take the A684 through Wensleydale to Bainbridge. Cross the river (signpost, Askrigg) and immediately after going round a sharp right-hand bend turn left (small signpost, Helm) up a narrow lane that goes up steeply into open countryside to the hamlet of Helm.

HELM COUNTRY HOUSE
Owners: Barbara & John Drew
Helm, Askrigg, near Leyburn
Yorkshire DL8 3JF, England
Tel & fax: (01969) 650443
www.karenbrown.com/england/helmcountryhouse.html
3 en-suite rooms
£34 per person, dinner £16
Closed Nov to Jan 2, , Credit cards: MC, VS
Children over 10, No-smoking house

Cobblestones border the main street of Helperby, a village where the number of shops (four) just outnumbers the pubs. Fronting onto the narrow lane that leads to the church, Brafferton Hall was built in the 1740s as the dower house to the much grander Helperby Hall. Now it is home to Sue and John White who find that their home's spacious, well-proportioned rooms are perfect for entertaining guests country-house style. Sue and John have an easy, friendly manner, so it is a pleasure to join them in the garden for pre-dinner drinks, dine with them, and chat afterwards over coffee and chocolates. (Sue thoughtfully feeds children an early supper so that they can be tucked up in bed by dinner time.) Upstairs, the spacious Garden Room has an en-suite bathroom with claw-foot tub. T's Room offers twin beds and a shower room while the smaller Pine Room, a double, is decked out with pine furniture with its bathroom down the hall. Sue finds the snug double room (with shower-room) perfect for singles or older children. Brafferton Hall is ideal for exploring not only the Yorkshire dales and moors, but also Rievaulx and Fountains abbeys, Castle Howard, Whitby, and York. *Directions:* Leave the A1 at Boroughbridge and follow the Easingwold road to Helperby. Turn right at the junction and right again up Hall Lane: Brafferton Hall is on your left after 100 yards.

BRAFFERTON HALL
Owners: Sue & John White
Helperby, York
Yorkshire Y06 2NZ, England
Tel & fax: (01423) 360352
www.karenbrown.com/england/braffertonhall.html
4 rooms, 3 en suite
£30 per person, dinner £18.50
Open all year, Credit cards: all major
Children welcome, No-smoking house
Wolsey Lodge

East Peterel Field Farm offers spectacular views of rolling countryside with hardly another building in sight, yet you are just over a mile from the delightful market town of Hexham, and 2 miles from Hadrian's Wall, the bleak, northernmost outpost of the Roman Empire. The glory of East Peterel Field Farm is its vast country kitchen where guests enjoy breakfast at the long trestle table in front of tall windows which frame the idyllic countryside views. Susan loves to cook, so specials such as salmon cakes and kedgeree are often served at breakfast time (she often gives cookery demonstrations or invites guest chefs to demonstrate their arts). Guests dine together round the dining-room table and are encouraged to bring their own wine to accompany their meal. If she has a large dinner party, Susan serves coffee in the lovely drawing room, but for smaller parties she utilizes the snug, a most attractive room full of comfortable chairs where a log fire bids a cheery welcome. The master bedroom is vast, the twin room lovely, and the small double has its bathroom just next door. David runs a small stud farm where he breeds and raises thoroughbreds—his dream is to breed a Derby winner. Hadrian's Wall is a great attraction hereabouts. The beautiful Northumbrian coast with all its castles is about a 40-mile drive away. *Directions:* From Hexham, turn into Blanchland Road, at the Tap and Spile pub, bear right at the Y for 1 mile, and take the first farm track to your right after the Black House restaurant.

EAST PETEREL FIELD FARM
Owners: Susan & David Carr
Hexham, Northumberland NE46 2JT, England
Tel: (01434) 607209, Fax: (01434) 601753
E-mail: bookings@petfield.demon.co.uk
www.karenbrown.com/england/eastpeterelfieldfarm.html
4 rooms, 2 en suite
£22–£28 per person, dinner £17.50
Open all year, Credit cards: none
Children over 1, No-smoking house

This timbered pink house and its black-painted wooden barn hug a quiet country road on the edge of the peaceful Suffolk village of Higham. Meg Parker, with her gentle dalmatian Crumpet at her heels, offers a warm smile and a sincere welcome to her home, quickly putting visitors at ease. Meg leads her guests to the lovely drawing room and then escorts them up the broad staircase to their rooms. Breakfast is enjoyed around the large dining-room table, and, since it is the only meal served, she is happy to offer advice on where to dine, often suggesting The Angel at Stoke by Nayland. Bedrooms vary in size from large twin-bedded rooms to a cozy double room, in the oldest part of the house, with an en-suite bathroom. Outside, Meg's large garden is carefully tended and stretches towards the River Brett where a punt and a canoe are available for guests' use. The narrow Brett soon becomes the broader Stour and you can punt/paddle upstream for a picnic and idly drift home or go downstream to Stratford St. Mary and work off a lunch at The Swan by making your way back upstream. An unheated swimming pool is tucked into one sheltered corner of the garden and a well-kept tennis court occupies another. A highlight of a stay here is to visit Flatford, immortalized in the paintings of John Constable. *Directions:* Leave the A12 between Colchester and Ipswich at Stratford St. Mary. The Old Vicarage is 1 mile to the west next to the church.

THE OLD VICARAGE
Owner: Meg Parker
Higham, Colchester
Suffolk CO7 6JY, England
Tel: (0120) 6337248, Fax: none
www.karenbrown.com/england/theoldvicaragehigham.html
3 rooms, 1 en suite
£25–£28 per person
Open all year, Credit cards: none
Children welcome
Wolsey Lodge

Manor Farm is a peaceful haven just inland from the sea, a glorious spot to enjoy once you have overcome the challenges of finding it. This part-whitewashed stone and slate manor is a splendid old building set in acres of glorious gardens. Muriel and Paul Knight operate on house party lines, with guests gathering for drinks and introductions at 6:30 pm and being shown into dinner at 7. While Muriel and Paul are warm and friendly, they tend to be a little more regimented than most, emphasizing that jacket and tie is a custom for gentlemen and stating that breakfast is served at 8:30 am sharp. With these few "rules" in mind, relax and enjoy your stay here in this lovely old antique-furnished house with its winter and summer lounges. Up one staircase are two lovely little cottagey rooms while up another are three equally delightful rooms. The scenery in this part of Cornwall is stunning and best enjoyed from the coastal path which meanders up and down the clifftops. Four miles away lies the strikingly picturesque harbor of Boscastle and just beyond it Tintagel with its legends of King Arthur. *Directions:* Ten miles south of Bude on the A39 turn right for Crackington Haven. At the sea front follow the same road up the other side of the valley and turn left into a narrow lane (Church Park Road) just before the red telephone box. Take the first right (Tinier lane) and Manor Farm is in front of you after 300 yards.

MANOR FARM   New
Owners: Muriel & Paul Knight
Higher Crackington, Crackington Haven
Nr Bude, Cornwall EX23 0JW, England
Tel: (01840) 230304, Fax: none
5 rooms, 4 en suite
£30 per person, dinner £15*
*Not available in August
Open all year, Credit cards: none
No Children, No-smoking house

Horsleygate Hall nestles in the sheltered Cordwell Valley at the edge of the Peak District National Park. The hall was built in 1783 as a farmhouse and later extended in 1836. Margaret and Robert have been careful to preserve all its old features such as the old farmhouse kitchen with its blackened Yorkshire range, flagstone floors, and the old pine woodwork and doors. Guests have a comfortable, homey sitting room and enjoy breakfast in the old schoolroom next door. Visitors often go to the Royal Oak in Millthorpe or the Robin Hood in Holmesfield for dinner. The attractive, spacious bedrooms enjoy views of the magnificent garden and superb Peak District scenery. The lovely garden contains many enchanting treasures: terraces, flower-filled borders, rock gardens, pools, and woodland paths. A grand garden on an infinitely larger scale surrounds Chatsworth House, the enormous home of the Duke and Duchess of Devonshire, which is full of opulent rooms and priceless paintings and furniture. Haddon Hall, a romantic, 14th-century manor house, has a fragrant rose garden. Bakewell, Ilam, Edensor, Hartington, Ashford-in-the-Water, and Eyam are particularly attractive villages in this area. *Directions:* Leave the M1 motorway at junction 29 into Chesterfield where you take the B6051 (Hathersage) through Barlow and Millthorpe, then take the first turn right (Horsleygate Lane) and immediately left into Horsleygate Hall's driveway.

HORSLEYGATE HALL
Owners: Margaret & Robert Ford
Horsleygate Lane
Holmesfield, near Chesterfield
Derbyshire S18 5WD, England
Tel: (0114) 2890333, Fax: none
3 rooms, 1 en suite
£19–£22.50 per person
Open all year, Credit cards: none
Children over 6, No-smoking house

The first thing you notice when you come through Woodhayes' front door is the portraits, huge paintings that sometimes stretch from floor to ceiling. Once you have made yourself at home in this friendly house, you may be inclined, as I was, to do a "who's who" of Noel's forbears, ascertaining how the congenial pictures in your room are related to all the others. Guests dine by candlelight round the polished dining-room table in what was at one time the home's kitchen—hence the flagstone floors and huge inglenook fireplace which now contains a wood-burning stove. The twin-bedded room at the front of the house has commanding views across the valley while the four-poster room overlooks the rose garden at the side of the house. Both have en-suite bathrooms. A single bedroom has its private bathroom down the hall. Dumpdon Celtic hill fort rises behind the house and beyond lies the rolling green of the Blackdown Hills, a wonderful place for walking. Nearby Honiton is the historic center for lace making and a small museum chronicles the industry's history and development. A 20-minute drive brings you to the Victorian resort of Sidmouth and Beer, a fishing village in a little bay. *Directions:* Woodhayes is prominently visible on high ground 1½ miles northeast of Honiton. Take the Dunkeswell road, cross the River Otter, and take the first turn right. Woodhayes' drive is the first on the left.

WOODHAYES
Owners: Christy & Noel Page-Turner
Honiton
Devon EX14 0TP, England
Tel & fax: (01404) 42011
www.karenbrown.com/england/woodhayes.html
3 rooms, 2 en suite
£32 per person, dinner £20
Closed Feb, Credit cards: MC, VS
Children over 15, Wolsey Lodge

The rector of Hopesay was quite the lord of the manor, with most of the building in this tiny hamlet falling under his domain: the 12th-century church of St. Mary, the grand 17th-century rectory, servants' cottages, stables, barns, and a school. Parishioners came from outlying farms and villages. However grand the former rector's lifestyle may have been, the house can never have looked lovelier than it does today. Relax by the log fire in the beautiful drawing room and admire the garden vista of mature copper beeches, Norway maples, azaleas, and rhododendrons. Enjoy a lovely dinner and breakfast round the long refectory table overlooking Hopesay Hill (NT). Equally delightful views are offered from the three very attractively decorated bedrooms. There are excellent country walks from the house and locally to Offa's dyke and the Long Mynd. Historical remains, hill forts, and castles abound (nearby Stokesay and Ludlow are a must). Guests often spend a day visiting the Ironbridge Gorge museums, while antiquers head to Ludlow and Shrewsbury. *Directions:* Leave the A49 at Craven Arms and take the B4368 to Clun. At Aston-on-Clun turn right over a small humpback bridge by the Flag Tree (literally a tree festooned with flags). The Old Rectory is on your left, next to the church, after 1 mile.

THE OLD RECTORY **New**
Owners: Roma & Michael Villar
Hopesay, nr Craven Arms
Shropshire SY7 8HD, England
Tel: (01588) 660245, Fax: (01588) 660502
3 en-suite rooms
£34 per person, dinner £20
Closed Christmas, Credit cards: none
Children over 12, No-smoking house

Sitting at the heart of the peaceful village of Hornton, the 17th-century Manor House is the exquisite home of Vicki and Malcolm Patrick and their three children. The elegant drawing room is set aside for guests' use and meals are taken in the beautifully appointed beamed dining room. Winter, decked out in soft tones of peach, is a delightful bedroom. Sweet peas decorate the bed linen in the Crow's Nest, an aptly named, snug attic room with exposed stone walls and a huge beam running across its floor. Across the courtyard, part of the stables has been converted into an adorable, two-bedroom, one-bath cottage which can be rented as self catering or on a bed-and-breakfast basis. Vicki is happy to prepare dinner when ordered in advance or directs guests to one of the numerous nearby village pubs that serve excellent food. Guests are welcome to swim in the swimming pool. Upton House, with its amazing collections of old masters paintings, Brussels tapestries, porcelain figures, and 18th-century furniture, is popular, as is the glorious Elizabethan home, Charlecote, and its surrounding park. *Directions:* From Banbury follow signposts for Stratford until you reach some traffic lights where the Stratford road goes left. Carry straight on the B4100 towards Warmington for half a mile then turn left for Horley and Hornton. In Horley turn right towards Hornton and in 2 miles turn left for Hornton. Drive down the hill and the manor house is on the left just past the post box on the verge and opposite the village school.

THE MANOR HOUSE
Owners: Vicki & Malcolm Patrick
The Green, Hornton, Banbury
Oxon OX15 6BZ, England
Tel & fax: (01295) 670386
www.karenbrown.com/england/themanorhouse.html
5 rooms, 2 en suite
£28.50–£32 per person, dinner £22.50
Open all year, Credit cards: none
Children welcome

Behind the tile-hung façade of Rixons lies a home that dates back to Tudor times, full of beams and low ceilings, with an inglenook fireplace and a snug, paneled study. Jean and Geoffrey dine with their visitors at the long refectory table, joining them afterwards for coffee and conversation round the fire. The galleried guestroom is open to the rafters with its bedroom downstairs and a sitting room and the bathroom on the balcony above. Honey-colored beams, country-pine furniture, and sprigged bedcovers make the twin-bedded room, tucked under the eaves, a delight. Horsted Keynes has a lovely old church built as a replica of one in Cahagnes, France by a Norman nobleman after the Battle of Hastings. By appointment you can visit The Forge, an adjacent museum containing artifacts of North American Plains Indians. On weekends and in the summer, vintage steam trains run between Horsted Keynes and Sheffield Park which is especially beautiful in spring. *Directions:* From the M25 take the M23 south, exiting at junction 10 on the A264 towards East Grinstead. At the second roundabout turn right on the B2028 and go about 6 miles through Ardingly. Take the left turning signposted Horsted Keynes and Danehill. In Horsted Keynes turn right into the Lewes Road—Rixons is the second house on the right.

RIXONS
Owners: Jean & Geoffrey Pink
Lewes Road
Horsted Keynes
West Sussex RH17 7DP, England
Tel: (01825) 790453
www.karenbrown.com/england/rixons.html
2 en-suite rooms
£28 per person, dinner £17.50
Closed Christmas & New Year
Credit cards: none
Children over 12, No-smoking house
Wolsey Lodge

Set in a valley carved by a stream rushing down from high, bleak moorlands, Hutton le Hole is a cluster of pale stone houses, a picturesque village in the heart of the spectacular North Yorkshire Moors National Park. The lintel above the Hammer and Hand's doorway declares the date of the house, built as a beer house for the iron workers, as 1784. Now it is home to Ann, a journalist, and John, once a London policeman, and their family who happily welcome guests to their guesthouse. Dinner is available every night, served in a small panelled dining room. The gentle tick of a huge grandfather clock and the crackle of a blazing log fire welcome you to the sitting room, where a television is available for guests' use. A steep, narrow staircase leads to three snug bedrooms, each prettily decorated. Additional bedrooms are found in the adjacent cottage. Hutton le Hole houses the Ryedale Folk Museum which is well worth a visit. York is less than an hour's drive away. *Directions:* Take the A170 from Thirsk towards Pickering. The left-hand turn to Hutton le Hole is signposted just after Kirbymoorside. The Hammer and Hand is at the heart of the village.

HAMMER AND HAND GUEST HOUSE
Owners: Ann & John Wilkins
Hutton le Hole
York
Yorkshire YO6 6UA, England
Tel: (01751) 417300, Fax: (01751) 417711
www.karenbrown.com/england/hamerandhand.html
5 en-suite rooms
£22 per person, dinner £12
Open all year, Credit cards: none
Children welcome, No-smoking house

A series of museums set along the wooded banks of a 5-mile stretch of the Severn river valley traces the history of the Industrial Revolution, for this was the Silicon Valley of the 18th century. The village of Ironbridge, stepping up the wooded hillside, grew up beside the first iron bridge in the world, built in 1779. Severn Lodge was once the village doctor's home—what used to be the patients' waiting room is now the guests' comfortable sitting room. Upstairs, the bedrooms are all beautifully decorated and kitted out with televisions, tea trays laid with fine china, and lots of information on what to do in the area. Two have their bath or shower rooms en suite while a third has its private bathroom across the hall. Breakfast, the only meal served, is taken either in the dining room or at a smaller table in the gracious hallway. There is no shortage of places nearby to enjoy an evening meal. A path leads from the garden down to the river and guests often walk to several of the museums. Attractions farther afield include stately homes such as Lord Bradford's Weston Park and the abbey at Much Wenlock. *Directions:* Leave the M54 at junction 4 and follow the brown signposts for the Ironbridge Gorge Museums and then the white signpost for the village of Ironbridge. With the river on your left, pass the iron bridge and take the first right (by The Malthouse pub) up New Road—Severn Lodge is on your right.

SEVERN LODGE
Owners: Nita & Alan Reed
New Road, Ironbridge
Shropshire TF8 7AS, England
Tel & fax: (01952) 432148
3 rooms, 2 en suite
£25 per person
Closed Dec 23 to 28, Credit cards: none
Children over 12, No-smoking house

Tim Earnshaw and Robin Martin have done an absolutely fabulous job of converting a traditional Yorkshire barn into a lovely home where beamed ceilings, stone features, antiques, comfortable furnishings, open fires, and a wholehearted welcome create a delightful atmosphere for guests. High Fold home is especially suitable for those who have trouble climbing stairs, for all but one of the bedrooms are on ground level and three of the bathrooms are handicapped friendly. While I loved the ground-floor bedrooms, Langcliffe, the upstairs room, won my heart—it has a small window that frames Langcliffe (the craggy bluff that rises above Kettlewell) and sheep grazing in the white stone-walled fields, and it also has a snug seating area offering countryside views. If you would like more privacy, or are travelling with children, opt to stay in the small self-contained lodge. Tim prepares a set four-course dinner and guests eat together round the old oak table. Walks abound in this lovely part of the Yorkshire Dales and one of the most popular passes right beside the barn. Car touring is just as enjoyable, offering castles, country homes, and abbeys. *Directions:* Kettlewell is in Wharfedale, 15 miles north of Skipton on the B6160. After crossing the main bridge into the village take the first turning right and next left to the King's Head pub. Take the road continuing in the same direction marked "for access only" and High Fold is on your right after 500 yards.

HIGH FOLD **New**
Owners: Tim Earnshaw & Robin Martin
Kettlewell, nr Skipton
Yorkshire BD23 5RJ, England
Tel: (01756) 760390, Fax: none
4 en-suite rooms
£27 per person, dinner £16
Open Mar to Dec, Credit cards: none
Children welcome

The magnificent scenery of the Lake District, the Yorkshire Dales, and Hadrian's Wall are within easy driving distance of Hipping Hall, so visitors can easily justify a stay of several days in Jocelyn Ruffle and Ian Bryant's comfortable home. (There are reduced half-board rates for guests staying more than one night.) Guests enjoy pre-dinner drinks in the conservatory which links the main part of the house to the Great Hall where dinner is served. A soaring, beamed ceiling and a broad-oak-plank floor provide an impressive setting for the excellent five-course meal served around one large table where guests are looked after by Ian while Jos creates in the kitchen. Ian selects wine to complement each course. The bedrooms are named after local hills and dales, and all are comfortably and very tastefully furnished, often with lovely old pieces bought at local auctions. Each has its own sparkling new, well-equipped bathroom. The 3 acres of garden are a delight and feature a large expanse of lawn set up for croquet and a kitchen garden which provides many of the vegetables enjoyed at dinner. Two suites, named Emily and Charlotte after the Brontë sisters who attended school in Cowan Bridge, occupy a courtyard cottage. They each have a kitchen and living room downstairs, bedroom and bathroom upstairs. *Directions:* Leave the M6 at junction 36 and follow the A65 through Kirkby Lonsdale towards Skipton. Hipping Hall is on the left, 3 miles after Kirkby Lonsdale.

HIPPING HALL
Owners: Jocelyn & Ian Bryant
Cowan Bridge
Kirkby Lonsdale
Cumbria LA6 2JJ, England
Tel: (015242) 71187, Fax: (015242) 72452
www.karenbrown.com/england/hippinghall.html
5 en-suite rooms & 2 suites
£43.50 per person, dinner £23
Open Mar to Nov, Credit cards: all major
Children over 12

As long ago as 1290 Penisale market was held here, but by the 1980s, all that was left of the community of Penisale was the shell of a farm and an ancient barn at the end of a rutted track. A local entrepreneur demolished the barn and incorporated its aged beams and stones into his vision of an Elizabethan farmhouse which he intended to be the center of a leisure complex. The venture went bankrupt and the house was purchased by Ann and Philip Unitt. They have done the most magnificent job of removing the "Las Vegas" aspects of the conversion and making this one of the premier bed-and-breakfast establishments in South Yorkshire. Splurge and request the Alderman's Suite and you're treated to a queen-sized bed set in an alcove beneath massive beams and a decadent bathroom complete with enormous tub. The three other bedrooms, one of which has a splendid four-poster bed, are small only by comparison. Dine in on the night of your arrival, as the manor is rather off the beaten track. Breakfast is usually served in the pine kitchen or the conservatory. The Peak District is on your doorstep and the countryside is very reminiscent of Brontë country which is about an hour's drive away. *Directions:* Leave the M1 at junction 35a and take the A616 (10 minutes) to the village of Midhopestones, just before Langsett village. Turn right to Penistone then at the next crossroads turn left—the manor is 1 mile down this road. When you see Brockholes Lane on the right, turn left and follow the farm track.

ALDERMAN'S HEAD MANOR
Owners: Ann & Philip Unitt
Hartcliffe Hill Road
Langsett, Stocksbridge
South Yorkshire S30 5GY, England
Tel & fax: (01226) 766209
4 rooms, 3 en suite
£22.50–£30 per person
Closed Christmas, Credit cards: VS
Children over 12, No-smoking house

Lavenham with its lovely timbered buildings, ancient guildhall, and spectacular church is the most attractive village in Suffolk. The Great House on the corner of the market square, a 15th-century building with an imposing 18th-century façade, houses a French restaurant-with-rooms run by Martine and Regis Crepy. Dinner is served in the oak-beamed dining room with candlelight and soft music and is particularly good value for money from Monday to Friday when a fixed-price menu is offered. On Saturday you dine from the à-la-carte menu and on Sunday evenings the restaurant is open only if guests are staying. In summer you can dine al fresco in the flower-filled courtyard. There are four large bedrooms, all with a lounge or a sitting area and bathroom. One has a second bedroom. Architecturally the rooms are divinely old-world, with sloping plank floors, creaking floorboards, little windows, and a plethora of beams. Enjoy the village in the peace and quiet of the evening after the throng of daytime summer visitors has departed. Next door, Little Hall is furnished in turn-of-the-century style and is open as a museum. Farther afield are other historic villages such as Kersey and Long Melford, and Constable's Flatford Mill. *Directions*: Lavenham is on the A1141 between Bury St. Edmunds and Hadleigh.

THE GREAT HOUSE
Owners: Martine & Regis Crepy
Market Place
Lavenham
Suffolk CO10 9QZ, England
Tel: (01787) 247431, Fax: (01787) 248007
4 en-suite rooms
£33–£44 per person, dinner £16.95
Closed Jan, Credit cards: all major
Children welcome

Buckton is a cluster of cottages and a couple of farms lining a quiet country lane on the outskirts of the pretty village of Leintwardine in the heart of the Marches, once an area of much inter-fiefdom feuding and armed conflict along the Welsh border. A 12th-century motte (mound) from a motte and bailey castle sits at the bottom of Yvonne and Hayden Lloyd's garden as evidence of the area's turbulent history. The substantial, tall Georgian farmhouse, very typical of those in this area, is a working farm with Hayden working with son Richard raising cattle and sheep and growing cereal. Three attractive bedrooms are found up the steep, broad flight of stairs. The double-bedded room has an en-suite shower room while the two twin-bedded rooms have their own private bathrooms across the hall. The Lloyds have an easy, welcoming way with guests that makes visitors feel very much a part of the family. Visiting castles is a popular pastime and they come in all shapes and sizes, from tiny Stokesay to the grandeur of Powys. Yvonne plans a route for guests through the unspoiled black and white timbered villages of adjacent Herefordshire. *Directions:* From Ludlow take the A49 north towards Shrewsbury for 3 miles and turn left on the A4113 towards Knighton. Cross the bridge in Leintwardine and take the first right (still A4113) to Walford (1 mile) where you turn right for Buckton. Follow the narrow lane and Upper Buckton is the second farm on the left.

UPPER BUCKTON   New
Owners: Yvonne & Hayden Lloyd
Buckton, Leintwardine, nr Craven Arms
Shropshire SY7 0JU, England
Tel: (01547) 540634, Fax: none
3 rooms, 1 en suite
£25 per person, dinner £18
Open all year, Credit cards: none
Children welcome, No-smoking house

Bed & Breakfast Descriptions   109

Tucked in an unspoilt valley high above the hustle and bustle of the more well-known Lake District tourist routes, this traditional pub lies surrounded by the ruggedly beautiful Lakeland scenery. Built of somber-looking slate in 1872 as a resting place for travelers, the hostelry is still a base for tourists, many of whom come here for the walking. They gather by the bar, the sound of their hiking boots echoing hollowly against the slate floor, poring over maps and discussing the day's activities. By contrast, the carpeted and curtained dining room and lounge with its velour chairs seem very sedate. The Stephenson family pride themselves on the quality of their food and offer a five-course meal in addition to substantial bar meals. Do not expect grand things of the accommodations as this is not a luxury establishment. However, for travelers who enjoy prettily decorated, simply furnished, and spotlessly clean rooms with modern bathrooms, the Three Shires fits the bill. Just a few miles away are some of the Lake District's most popular villages: Hawkshead, Ambleside, Coniston, and Grasmere. *Directions:* From Ambleside take the A593, Coniston road, cross Skelwith Bridge, and take the first right, signposted The Langdales and Wrynose Pass. Take the first left to Little Langdale and the Three Shires Inn is on your right.

THREE SHIRES INN
Owners: Stephenson family
Little Langdale
Ambleside
Cumbria LA22 9NZ, England
Tel: (015394) 37215, Fax: (015394) 37127
www.karenbrown.com/england/threeshiresinn.html
10 en-suite rooms
£27–£38 per person, dinner £17.957
Closed Jan, Credit cards: MC, VS
Children welcome

Built in 1673 as a rectory, Landewednack House sits above the 6th-century church and a cluster of cottages which lead down to the rocky inlet of Church Cove at the tip of the Lizard Peninsula, the southernmost spot in England. Restored to a state of luxury unknown to former residents, Landewednack House was purchased by Marion and Peter Stanley who fell in love with the house, its walled garden, and magnificent views. Guests are welcomed with a traditional Cornish tea of scones, clotted cream, and strawberry jam served in the elegant sitting room or secluded garden. In the evening guests may dine together in the dining room before a log fire in the massive 17th-century fireplace or separately in the beamed morning room. The starched linen coverlets on the polished mahogany half-tester bed in the Yellow Room present a dramatic picture in a room whose floor-to-ceiling bay window frames a lovely view of the garden and the church silhouetted against the sea. Choose the Red Room for its 18th-century four-poster bed or the Chinese Room for its silk-draped king-sized bed that can also be twins. Walk along the clifftops to the adorable village of Cadgwith or visit the many beautiful Cornish gardens and return to soak in the Jacuzzi. *Directions:* From Helston, take the A3083 to Lizard (do **not** turn right at the first Church Cove sign near Helston). Turn left before entering the village, signposted Church Cove. Take the next left (Church Cove and Lifeboat Station) and Landewednack is on the left.

LANDEWEDNACK HOUSE
Owners: Marion & Peter Stanley
Church Cove, Lizard, Helston
Cornwall TR12 7PQ, England
Tel: (01326) 290909, Fax: (01326) 290192
3 rooms, 2 en suite
£34–£42 per person, dinner £21
Closed Christmas, Credit cards: MC, VS
Children not accepted, No-smoking house
Wolsey Lodge

The village of Llanmynech straddles the border between Wales and England, making it the perfect location for exploring both Shropshire and North Wales. In order to make their home more spacious, Carol and Bryan Fahey have combined two small front rooms into a guest dining and sitting room with a log fire for colder weather. The house was for many years the village dame school and a photo of the class of 1904 hangs in the hallway. Up the narrow staircase are three attractive bedrooms—one double/twin room has its own en-suite shower room, while the other double is large enough to accommodate a lovely Victorian half-tester bed. The latter room and the twin bedroom have their own private facilities. As a retired catering lecturer, Carol offers a high standard of cuisine at moderate cost, which she feels contributes to her having so many return guests. Bryan, a keen fly-fisherman, is happy to give advice and make fishing arrangements for guests. The Faheys are keen walkers, as are many of their guests who come to hike along Offa's Dyke and enjoy walking beside the Montgomery Canal. A lovely day out in Wales could include visiting Llanrhaeder waterfall and a drive around Lake Vyrnwy. *Directions:* From Oswestry, take the A483 towards Welshpool for 5½ miles to the village of Llanmynech. Turn left on the B4398 toward Knockin and after ¼ mile cross the humpback bridge: Vyrnwy Bank is the fourth house on the left.

VYRNWY BANK
Owners: Carol & Bryan Fahey
Llanmynech
Shropshire SY22 6LG, England
Tel: (01691) 830427, Fax: none
3 rooms, 1 en suite
£16–£20 per person, dinner £9
Closed Feb, Credit cards: none
Children welcome

When the Richards bought this house they were unaware that their cottage-style home with its maze of little rooms was in fact a medieval great hall with giant wooden beams and roof trusses. Careful restoration has revealed the large parlor below and the great hall above. While the parlor with its mullioned windows, beamed ceiling, and sofas arranged before the huge stone fireplace causes guests to "ooh and aah," it is the great hall that makes them gasp as they regard the massive roof trusses and the maze of intricate timberwork soaring overhead. The soft glow of flickering candlelight bathes guests as they dine at the refectory table in the great hall. Cozy, beamed bedrooms are decorated to perfection in country-print fabrics and have accompanying bathrooms neatly tucked under the rafters. The garden, which is completely encircled by a wide moat, has a willow-shaded fish pond which is home to lazily swimming ducks. Nearby Shrewsbury with its twisting lanes, castle, and open-pillared market hall deserves exploration. Farther afield are the Ironbridge Gorge Museum and the historic town of Ludlow. *Directions:* From Shrewsbury take the A49 south for 8 miles: Longnor is signposted to the left. Go through the village past the school and turn left into the lane marked "No Through Road." When the lane turns left, Moat House is straight ahead.

MOAT HOUSE
Owners: Margaret & Peter Richards
Longnor
Shrewsbury
Shropshire SY5 7PP, England
Tel & fax: (01743) 718434
2 en-suite rooms
£35 per person, dinner £21
Open Apr to Oct, Credit cards: MC, VS
Children not accepted

John claims that he would still be wandering the world (something he had done for over three years) if he had not met Hazel who brought him back to live in the Lake District valley where she was raised. Together they have restored a roadside farm, providing guest accommodation in the farmhouse and stables and transforming the barn into a tea room and restaurant. Flagstone floors, beamed ceilings, and old fireplaces are the order of the day in the farm. Hazel prepares a set, four-course dinner, but if you prefer a lighter, less formal meal, walk across to the barn where little tables and chairs are arranged in the old cow stalls, specials are posted on the board, and main courses include quiche, fish, and steak. Upstairs two of the country-cozy bedrooms offer zip-link beds and en-suite bathrooms while the other two are snug double-bedded rooms with en-suite shower rooms. All have delightful countryside views. My favorite room lies a few steps from the house in the former stables—its ground floor location makes it ideal for those who have difficulty with stairs. New House Farm sits amid the rugged scenery which has made the Lake District such a draw for centuries. Follow the country lane to Crummock Water and Buttermere from where the road winds and twists over the fells to Rosthwaite, Grange, and Keswick. *Directions:* From exit 40 on the M6 take the A66 past Keswick, and turn left onto the B5292 to Lorton. Follow signs for Buttermere and New House Farm is on your left after half a mile.

NEW HOUSE FARM
Owners: Hazel & John Hatch
Lorton near Cockermouth
Cumbria CA13 9UU, England
Tel & fax: (01900) 85404
www.karenbrown.com/england/newhousefarm.html
5 en-suite rooms
£30–£40 per person, dinner £20
Open all year, Credit cards: none
Children over 12, No-smoking house

This endearing cottage dates back to the early 14th century when it was home to a yeoman farmer. With its little upstairs windows peeking out from beneath a heavy thatch roof and its timber-framed wall fronted by a flower-filled garden, Loxley Farm presents an idyllic picture. The picture-book ambiance is continued inside where guests breakfast together round a long table in the low-beamed dining room. Accommodation is across the garden in the converted 17th-century thatched, half-timbered cart barn with two suites, the Hayloft Suite, with vaulted ceilings, bedroom, bathroom, sitting room, and small kitchen, and the Garden Suite, with bedroom, bathroom, and garden room whose semi-circular glass walls look over the orchard, lawns, and house. Breakfast is the only meal served in the farmhouse dining room and guests often walk into Loxley to dine or go to The Bell in Alderminster. A quiet back road brings you into the center of Stratford-upon-Avon (4 miles). Here there are historical timbered buildings to investigate, lovely shops, and the Royal Shakespeare Theatre. In nearby Shottery is Anne Hathaway's picture-book cottage. Warwick Castle and Coventry Cathedral are both easily visited from Loxley. *Directions:* Loxley is signposted off the A422 Stratford-upon-Avon to Banbury road about 4 miles from Stratford on the left. Go through the village to the bottom of the hill, turn left (Stratford-upon-Avon), and Loxley Farm is the third house on the right.

LOXLEY FARM
Owners: Anne & Rod Hornton
Loxley
Warwickshire CV35 9JN, England
Tel & fax: (01789) 840265
www.karenbrown.com/england/loxleyfarm.html
2 en-suite rooms
£25–£27.50 per person
Closed Christmas & New Year, Credit cards: none
Children welcome

Set in a sheltered valley in the center of Exmoor National Park, this farm complex comprises several 14th-century barns and a 200-year-old farmhouse set round a cobbled courtyard. Hens, guinea fowl, and peacocks complete the idyllic countryside picture. Three very nice bedrooms are found in the sturdy farmhouse: the attractive twin-bedded room is my favorite because of its spaciousness, airy decor, two comfortable armchairs, and lovely countryside views. The same view is shared by the adjacent four-poster room, while a small double-bedded room is found at the back of the house. If you are traveling with younger children, you might want to stay on a bed-and-breakfast basis in one of the self-catering cottages in the ancient barns. Ann provides a set three-course candlelit dinner and guests are welcome to bring their own wine to accompany their meal. Guests can fish in the Durbins' trout lake or go salmon-fishing on the nearby Exe and Barle rivers. Exmoor has delightful little unspoilt villages nestling in wooded valleys, rugged moorlands where sheep and ponies graze, and a coastline with the delightful seaside towns of Lynton and Lynmouth and the quaint little village of Porlock Weir. *Directions:* Exit the M5 at junction 25, take the A358 (Minehead road) for 5 miles, bypassing Bishops Lydeard, and turn left on the B3224 to Wheddon Cross. Go straight across the main street of the village and Cutthorne is on your left after 3 miles.

CUTTHORNE
Owners: Ann & Philip Durbin
Luckwell Bridge, Wheddon Cross
Somerset TA24 7EW, England
Tel & fax: (01643) 831255
www.karenbrown.com/england/cutthorne.html
3 en-suite rooms, 2 cottages
£23–£27 per person, dinner £12.50
Open mid-Feb to mid-Nov, Credit cards: none
Children over 12 in house, any age in cottages
No-smoking house

The Salweys of Shropshire can trace their lineage hereabouts back to 1216 and The Lodge has been in their family since it was built in the early 1700s, but it is definitely not a formal place. Hermione puts guests at ease, encouraging them to feel as though they are friends of the family, and enjoys pointing out the architectural details of the house and explaining who's who amongst the family portraits. In the evening, guests gather in the morning room and help themselves to drinks from the honesty bar before going into dinner at a spectacular long table made of burled wood, made especially for the house. Up the grand staircase the three large bedrooms are most attractive: Chinese has a suite of furniture painted in an Asian motif, Roses is a large double with an enormous bathroom, and The Yellow Room is a large twin with its bathroom across the hall. The large garden, woodland, and farmland make this an ideal place for walking. The nearest tourist attraction is the medieval town of Ludlow with its old inns, alleyways of antique shops, Norman castle, and riverside walks. *Directions:* Leave Ludlow over Ludford Bridge traveling south. After 1½ miles turn right on the B4361 signposted Richards Castle. After 400 yards turn right through the entrance gates of The Lodge by a curved stone wall, and continue up the long drive to the house.

THE LODGE
Owners: Hermione & Humphrey Salwey
Ludlow
Shropshire SY8 4DU, England
Tel: (01584) 872103, Fax: (01584) 876126
3 rooms, 2 en suite
£35 per person, dinner £20 (wine included)
Open Apr to Oct, Credit cards: none
Children not accepted, No-smoking house
Wolsey Lodge

Ludlow is a charming, compact town of cobbled stone streets rising from the River Teme to its immense Norman Castle, and the most delightful street in town is the splendid upsweep of Lower Broad Street which narrows to the 13th-century Broadgate, the only surviving gatehouse. The architecture of Lower Broad Street runs the gamut from Tudor, through Georgian to Victorian and this Number Twenty Eight offers you a house of each style, with two en-suite bedrooms in each house. Number Twenty Eight itself is a Georgian—you step directly from the street into a cozy parlor with an open fire, book-lined walls, prints, plates, and pictures, and a warm welcome from Patricia and Philip Ross. Guests congregate here for breakfast which in summer is served on the flower-filled terrace. If you are staying up the road, you have your choice of eating here or preparing yourself a Continental breakfast from your well-stocked refrigerator. Broadgate Mews is two tiny Tudor cottages combined to form a secluded haven, while the delightful Westview is a restored Victorian terrace home offering especially nice bedrooms with brass and wrought-iron beds and spacious, very up-to-date bathrooms. Explore the immense Norman castle and wander the lanes with their fine period houses and plethora of book and antique shops. *Directions:* Arriving from the south, fork left off the A49 onto the B4361 signposted Ludlow south and Richards Castle. Cross the river and go straight into Lower Broad Street. There is unrestricted parking on the street.

NUMBER TWENTY EIGHT   **New**
Owners Patricia & Philip Ross
Lower Broad Street
Ludlow, Shropshire SY5 1PQ, England
Tel: (01584) 876996, Fax: (01584) 87680
E-mail: ross.no28@btinternet.com
6 en-suite rooms
£30 per person
Open all year, Credit cards: MC, VS
Children welcome, No-smoking house

How unusual to find an outstanding Elizabethan manor amidst the suburbs and how lucky that this manor is a 15-minute drive from Heathrow airport, making it absolutely perfect for a few nights at the beginning or end of your stay in England if you are visiting from overseas. Carved faces by the massive front door, bowed leaded windows, paneling, and beams make this the most impressive of homes where the warmest of welcomes is offered by Bar and her sister Sue. Relax in the oak-paneled sitting room or curl up in the upstairs hallway nook with a cup of tea and biscuits. Bedrooms are delightful: the large paneled double has an en-suite shower, the twin is decorated in sunny lemons and has its bathroom across the hall, and the small double room has a little sitting area in the tall bay window which overlooks the lovely garden. For dinner guests often walk to the pub down the road. Maidenhead railway station is only a mile away and a 30-minute train ride finds you in London—ideal for the theater or sightseeing. Windsor, Henley on Thames, and Marlow are a 15-minute drive away, while Oxford is 45 minutes away. *Directions:* Leave the M4 at junction 8/9 and take the A404 (M) to junction 9A signposted Cox Green. Follow the Cox Green signs at both mini-roundabouts into Cox Green Road. Turn left at the Foresters pub and Beehive Manor is on your right in 600 yards.

BEEHIVE MANOR
Owners: Bar Barbour & Sue Lemin
Cox Green Lane
Maidenhead
Berkshire SL6 3ET, England
Tel: (01628) 620980, Fax: (01628) 621840
www.karenbrown.com/england/beehivemanor.html
3 rooms, 2 en suite
£29 per person
Closed Christmas, Credit cards: none
Children over 12, No-smoking house

Set in the gently rolling countryside of the Yorkshire Wolds between York and the North York Moors National Park, Newstead Grange is ideally located for exploring these popular tourist destinations and the coastal towns of Whitby and Scarborough. Pat and Paul Williams forsook their careers as teachers to purchase a spacious Georgian home and open it as a bed and breakfast. Guests have two comfortable sitting rooms, one resplendent with grand piano in the large bay-window overlooking the garden. Pat enjoys cooking and while there are no choices on her daily menu, she tries to avoid foods guests dislike. Many of her vegetables come from the large garden. Upstairs the bedrooms, all named after former owners, range in size from the spaciousness of Pickering with its half tester bed and Wertheimer to two very snug little rooms in a tiny cottage annexed to the house. Castle Howard is just 8 miles away—one look at its immense façade reflecting in a broad lake and you can understand why it took 27 years to build. It isn't really a castle at all but one of England's grandest homes, as impressive inside as out, full of fine furniture and paintings. There is also a wealth of more intimate less imposing homes to visit such as Sledmere House near Malton and Duncombe Park in nearby Helmsley. *Directions:* Follow signs for Beverley (B1248) out of Malton and ½ a mile beyond the last houses you find Newstead Grange on your left opposite a road sign for Settrington.

NEWSTEAD GRANGE　New
Owners: Pat & Paul Williams
Beverley Road, Norton on Derwent
Malton, Yorkshire YO17 9PJ, England
Tel: (01653) 692502, Fax: (01653) 696951
8 en-suite rooms
£34.50–£36.50 per person, dinner £16.50
Open Mar to Sep, Credit cards: MC, VS
Children over 10, No-smoking house

Conjecture has it that Thomas Hardy used Old Lamb House (then the Lamb Inn) as Rollivers Tavern in *Tess of the d'Urbervilles*. Jenny and Ben continue the tradition of hospitality by offering accommodation to guests in two large front bedrooms which share a bathroom. Guests use the front door (while family use the kitchen door) and atop the curving staircase there's a sitting area with two armchairs and lots of tourist information. Jenny finds that most guests prefer to relax in their bedrooms, both of which contain comfortable, old-fashioned armchairs. The Pink Room is decked out in soft pinks with matching flowery bed-linen and drapes, while the Gray Room is outfitted in soft blue-grays and offers lovely views of the garden with its stately cedar tree. Guests usually drive the short distance to the Crown or the Blackmore Vale pubs for dinner. Alternatively, there are several restaurants nearby. Dorset abounds in country lanes that lead to pretty villages such as Milton Abbas and Cerne Abbas with its club-wielding giant carved into the chalk hillside. Shaftesbury has many steep roads running down into Blackmore Vale, the most famous being cobbled Gold Hill. *Directions:* From Shaftesbury take the A30 towards Exeter for 4 miles to East Stour. Turn left on B3092 to Marnhull (3 miles) and go half a mile beyond Marnhull church where you turn right at the triangle of grass with a signpost and into Old Lamb House's driveway.

OLD LAMB HOUSE
Owners: Jenny & Ben Chilcott
Marnhull
Dorset DT10 1QG, England
Tel: (01258) 820491, Fax: (01258) 821464
E-mail: ben@bcaviation.demon.co.uk
www.karenbrown.com/england/oldlambhouse.html
2 rooms, neither en suite
£20 per person
Closed Christmas & New Year, Credit cards: none
Children welcome, No-smoking house

Middleham is an attractive town of gray-stone houses sitting beneath the ruins of Middleham Castle. Separated from the cobbled market square by a rose garden, Waterford House is much older than its Victorian exterior suggests. Built as a substantial family home, the house was in recent times divided into two by a husband and wife who wished to live apart but remain in the same village. Now, happily, it is a single house again and the only reminder of its days as two homes are the stairways at either side of the house that lead to the bedrooms. These delightful bedrooms, two of which are four-posters, all have an en-suite shower, and are furnished, as is the entire house, with lovely old furniture and Everyl and Brian's collections of all things old and interesting. A double room has an extra bed and families with two children appreciate the bunk beds tucked neatly into the corner. An integral part of your stay here is sampling the delicious dinners that Everyl prepares and serves in the antique-packed dining room. The dinner menu changes slightly every night and completely every week and you can dine à la carte or choose an evening-long five-course dinner. Waterford House is an ideal central location for exploring the Yorkshire dales. *Directions:* Leave the A1 on the B6267 to Masham and on to Middleham. Waterford House is on your left (on the Leyburn road) just beyond the town's cobbled square.

WATERFORD HOUSE
Owners: Everyl & Brian Madell
19 Kirkgate
Middleham
Yorkshire DL8 4PG, England
Tel & fax: (01969) 622090 or Fax: (01969) 624020
www.karenbrown.com/england/waterfordhouse.html
5 en-suite rooms
£32.50–£42.50 per person, dinner £19.50–£27.50
Open all year, Credit cards: VS
Children welcome

Mungrisdale is one of the few unspoilt villages left in the Lake District and is made up of a pub, an old church, and a cluster of houses and farms set at the foot of rugged, gray-blue crags. Do not confuse The Mill with the adjoining pub, The Mill Inn: drive through the car park of the inn to reach private parking for this cozy hotel. Rooms are of cottage proportions: a small lounge with comfy chairs gathered round a blazing log fire, a cozy dining room where each small oak table is set with blue napkins, candles, willow-pattern china, and a tiny flower arrangement, and nine small bedrooms with matching draperies and bedspreads. Most visitors are drawn here for the dinners prepared by Eleanor. Dinner consists of an appetizer followed by a tasty homemade soup served with soda bread (the latter a popular fixture on the menu), a main course (with a vegetarian alternative), dessert, and cheese and biscuits. Bookings only for bed and breakfast are not usually accepted. The Lake District is a beautiful region, popular with walkers and sightseers alike. Some of its premier villages are Coniston, Hawkshead, Sawrey (home of Beatrix Potter), Ambleside, and Grasmere. *Directions:* Leave the M6 at junction 40 and take the A66 towards Keswick for 10 miles. The Mill is 2 miles north of this road and the signpost for Mungrisdale is midway between Penrith and Keswick.

THE MILL HOTEL
Owners: Eleanor & Richard Quinlan
Mungrisdale
Penrith
Cumbria CA11 0XR, England
Tel: (017687) 79659, Fax: (017687) 79155
www.karenbrown.com/england/themillhotel.html
9 rooms, 7 en suite
£49–£61 per person dinner, B & B
Open Mar to Oct, Credit cards: none
Children welcome

In her younger years Beatrix Potter used to visit Ees Wyke House with her family. Now it is a very pleasant hotel run by Mag and John Williams who have painted and decorated the house from top to bottom in a comfortable style. John, a former cookery teacher at a catering college, enjoys cooking and his dinner menu always offers choices of starter, main course, and dessert. Dinner is taken in the large dining room with glorious views across the countryside. The bedrooms have tall windows framing gorgeous countryside views and many overlook nearby Esthwaite Water. Tucked under the eaves, two airy, spacious attic bedrooms have super views: one has a bathroom en suite while the other has a private bath just next door. The other bedrooms also have a mix of en-suite and adjacent bathroom arrangements. The smallest bedroom, on the ground floor, is reserved for visitors who have difficulty with stairs but unfortunately has no view. A short stroll up the village brings you to Hill Top Farm where Beatrix Potter wrote several of her books. Walks abound in the area and the more oft-trod Lakeland routes are easily accessible by taking the nearby ferry across Lake Windermere. *Directions:* From Ambleside take the A593 towards Coniston. After about a mile turn left on the B5286 to Hawkshead. Skirt Hawkshead village and follow signs for the ferry. Ees Wyke House is on the right just before Sawrey.

EES WYKE COUNTRY HOUSE HOTEL
Owners: Mag & John Williams
Near Sawrey
Hawkshead, Ambleside
Cumbria LA22 0JZ, England
Tel & fax: (015394) 36393
www.karenbrown.com/england/eeswykecountryhousehotel.html
8 rooms, 6 en suite
£56 per person dinner bed & breakfast
Open Mar to Dec, Credit cards: AX
Children over 10 & babies

The quiet, narrow country lane that runs in front of Fosse Farmhouse is the historical Fosse Way, the road built by the Romans to connect their most important forts from Devon to Lincolnshire. Caron Cooper has furnished her rooms with great flair using soft colors and enviable country-French antiques in every room. Charming collectibles and country china adorn much of the sitting and breakfast rooms and most pieces are for sale. Upstairs there are three extremely comfortable guest bedrooms. My favorite was The Pine Room with its mellow pine furniture and especially spacious, luxuriously equipped bathroom. Across the courtyard, the ground floor of the stables has been converted to a tea room and restaurant. On the floor above, three cottage-style bedrooms are stylishly decorated in white on white. With advance notice, Caron enjoys preparing an imaginative, three-course dinner, and is happy to cater to vegetarian palates. At Christmas Caron offers a three-day festive holiday. This tranquil countryside setting is within an easy half-hour's drive of Bath, Bristol, Tetbury, and Cirencester, and the picture-perfect village of Castle Combe is also nearby. *Directions:* Exit the M4 at junction 17 towards Chippenham, turn right on the A420 (Bristol road) for 3 miles to the B4039 which you take around Castle Combe to The Gib where you turn left opposite The Salutation Inn. Fosse Farmhouse is on your right after 1 mile.

FOSSE FARMHOUSE
Owner: Caron Cooper
Nettleton Shrub, Nettleton, Chippenham
Wiltshire SN14 7NJ, England
Tel: (01249) 782286, Fax: (01249) 783066
E-mail: 100547.2030@compuserve.com
www.karenbrown.com/england/fossefarmhouse.html
6 en-suite rooms
£45–£65 per person, dinner £23
Open all year, Credit cards: all major
Children welcome

Sitting at the head of Wensleydale, Newton le Willows is a very quiet village off the beaten track—a cluster of houses, a pub, and The Hall, home to Oriella Featherstone. Oriella is just as flamboyant as her name suggests and her house is decorated like herself, in a graciously extravagant manner. Artfully draped curtains cascading to the floors hang from all the windows and many of the doors. Sofas are piled with plump cushions, plants trail from pots, and grand flower arrangements grace lovely pieces of furniture, while the dining table is set in the evening with silver service enhanced by twinkling candlelight. Relax in the comfortable drawing room or curl up by the fire in the intimate snug. Oriella has five bedrooms though she never takes more than six guests. All are decorated lavishly and vary in size from spacious to grand (the suite that spans the house). Nearby eating places offer food ranging from inexpensive to some of the best you will find in Britain. Within a half hour's drive of this lovely part of Yorkshire are Middleham with its racing stables and ruined castle of Richard II, Bolton Castle where Mary Queen of Scots was held captive, and the ruins of Jervaulx, and Fountains abbeys. *Directions:* Leave the A1 at Leeming Bar taking the A684 to Bedale. At the main street turn right and half a mile out of town take the first left, signposted Newton le Willows. Continue to T junction and turn right. At the Wheatsheaf Inn turn left and right into The Hall's driveway.

THE HALL   *New*
Owner: Oriella Featherstone
Newton le Willows, nr Bedale
Yorkshire DL8 1SW, England
Tel: (01677) 450210, Fax: (01677) 450014
5 en-suite rooms
£40–£45 per person, dinner £20
Open all year, Credit cards: none
Children over 13

This 17th-century former woolen mill deep in the heart of the Devon countryside is now the most welcoming of casual country hotels run with great style by Hazel Phillips and Peter Hunt. It's an informal spot where Peter greets you in the flagstoned hallway and shows you up to your room, encouraging you to make yourself thoroughly at home. After a drink in the bar when Peter passes out the menus, with three choices for each of the three courses, you are shown into the little dining room with its pine tables and chairs set before a massive inglenook fireplace. Upstairs all but one of the cozy bedrooms have snug bathrooms or showers en suite. Peter is an avid beekeeper after sampling his honey for breakfast, guests often purchase a pot to enjoy back home. Peter's other great interest is his flock of Jacob sheep—woolen garments "fresh from the flock" are often for sale. It's a tremendous place to relax and unwind: sit on the lawn and listen to the burble of the River Bovey flowing alongside, or walk along the river the rivers and up on the moors. Birdwatching is a great attraction here. Drogo Castle is just up the road and all the varied delights of Dartmoor National Park on your doorstep. *Directions:* From Exeter take the A38 to the A382, Bovey Tracy, turnoff. Turn left in Moretonhampstead onto the Princetown road, then immediately left again to North Bovey. Go straight through the village down the hill and take the first right for the ¼-mile drive to Blackaller.

BLACKALLER   New
Owners: Hazel Phillips & Peter Hunt
North Bovey, Devon TQ13 8QY, England
Tel & fax: (01647) 440322 (phone to arrange to fax)
5 rooms, 4 en suite
£32–£36 per person, dinner £21
Open Mar to Dec, Credit cards: none
Children welcome

Set in the picturesque moorland village of North Bovey, frequent winner of the best kept Dartmoor village award, Gate House has a lovely location just behind the tree-lined village green. The location and warm welcome offered by hosts Sheila and John Williams add up to the perfect recipe for a countryside holiday. The sitting room has an ancient bread oven tucked inside a massive granite fireplace beneath a low, beamed ceiling, and the adjacent dining room has a pine table in front of an atmospheric old stove. A narrow stairway leads up from the dining room to two of the guest bedrooms, each with a neat bathroom tucked under the eaves. The third bedroom is found at the top of another little staircase, this one off the sitting room, and affords views through a huge copper beech to the swimming pool (unheated) which guests are welcome to use, and idyllic green countryside. Sheila prepares a lovely country breakfast and a four-course evening meal (including vegetarian dishes if requested). Apart from walking on the moor and touring the moorland villages, guests enjoy visiting the many nearby National Trust properties. The Devon coastline is easily accessible and many guests take a day trip into Cornwall, often venturing as far afield as Clovelly. *Directions:* From Exeter take the A38 to the A382, Bovey Tracy, turnoff. Turn left in Mortenhampstead onto the Princetown road, then immediately left again to North Bovey. Go down the lane into the village and Gate House is on the left beyond the Ring of Bells.

GATE HOUSE
Owners: Sheila & John Williams
North Bovey
Devon TQ13 8RB, England
Tel & fax: (01647) 440479
www.karenbrown.com/england/gatehouse.html
3 en-suite rooms
£25 per person, dinner £14
Open all year, Credit cards: none
Children over 15

Rectory Farm was purchased by Robert's grandparents in 1915. While Robert continues the family farming tradition, his wife Mary Anne offers bed-and-breakfast accommodation in their lovely Elizabethan farmhouse. Mary Anne and Robert have put a lot of effort into tastefully modernizing and refurbishing their very old home. Guests have a small sitting and breakfast room with a woodburning stove. Upstairs, a modern shower room has been added to the large twin-bedded room where you sleep beneath an unusual ceiling whose support beam is covered in decorative plasterwork. A lovely fireplace was unearthed in this room during remodeling. A smaller pine double bedroom has an en-suite shower room and sits among the family's bedrooms. Breakfast is the only meal served, so guests often enjoy dinner at the Red Lion pub in the village or the many other excellent eating places nearby. The farmlands border the River Thames where you can walk along the towpath and go fishing. An hour's drive will find you in Stratford-upon-Avon or Bath. Closer at hand, you can tour the Oxford colleges, try your hand at punting, and visit Blenheim Palace where Churchill was born. *Directions:* From Oxford, take the A420 (Swindon) to Kingston Bagpuize, turn right on the A415 (Witney), cross the river and turn immediately right beside the Rose Revived car park. After 2 miles turn right at the T-junction, and Rectory Farm is on the right beside the church.

RECTORY FARM
Owners: Mary Anne & Robert Florey
Northmoor
Witney
Oxfordshire OX8 1SX, England
Tel: (01865) 300207, Fax: (01865) 300559
www.karenbrown.com/england/rectoryfarm.html
2 en-suite rooms
£20–£22 per person
Open Feb to mid-Dec, Credit cards: none
Children over 14, No-smoking house

The Grange, a former rectory, is a rambling Regency home covered with wisteria, and comfortably furnished by Sue and Malcolm Whittley. Guests are welcome to use the cozy television room or the formal drawing room overlooking the vast expanses of sweeping lawn and mature trees. The five bedrooms range in size from a large twin room softly carpeted in pink with light-pink walls and cushioned window seats, to a compact double room with sunny yellow walls, prettily furnished in country pine. Homey touches such as hanging bouquets of dried flowers, pictures on the walls, and even a Paddington bear on a corner shelf add warmth. Amidst the 5 acres of lawns and gardens, tucked behind the kitchen garden and beyond the ducks and peacocks, is a walled swimming pool. Northwold is within easy reach of Norwich with its splendid castle museum and cathedral, the ancient university town of Cambridge, the medieval market town of King's Lynn, and the unspoilt, scenic north Norfolk coast. Nearby are the Royal Family's summer home, Sandringham House, the Caley Mill lavender farm, and the church in Heacham where John Rolfe married his Indian princess, Pocohontas. *Directions:* From King's Lynn take the A134, signposted Thetford, to Northwold. Turn left into the village, pass the church and the Old Rectory (on the left), and turn left in front of the row of cottages which brings you into The Grange's driveway.

THE GRANGE
Owners: Sue & Malcolm Whittley
Northwold
Thetford
Norfolk IP26 5NF, England
Tel: (01366) 728240, Fax: (01366) 728005
www.karenbrown.com/england/thegrange.html
5 rooms, 2 en suite
£18–£22.50 per person, dinner £13
Closed Christmas, Credit cards: none
Children welcome

The main attraction of Norton St. Philip, aside from its lovely old cottages, is the magnificent George pub, a grand old-fashioned hostelry that has been offering hospitality to travelers for many hundreds of years. Just up the High street, sheltered from the street by large garden and the adjacent warehouse by a thick screen of trees, you find Monmouth House, home to Traudle and Leslie Graham. The entrance hall opens up to an extremely comfortable open-plan sitting and dining room with tall windows framing the well-tended garden and countryside views to the distant Mendip Hills. Guests eat together round the long dining-room table where breakfast is the only meal served. For dinner The George and the Fleur de Lys serve good food in congenial surroundings. The spacious ground floor bedrooms have all benefited from Traudle's handiwork: not only has she decorated the rooms and sewn the drapes, she has tiled their spacious bath and shower rooms. Norton St. Philip is an ideal location for visiting Georgian Bath with its wealth of attractions and Wells with its magnificent cathedral set in spacious grounds. During the quiet evening hours you can follow a walking tour that leads you round the village. *Directions:* Leave Bath on the A37 (Exeter road). At the top of the dual carriageway turn left for Frome (B3110) for the 7 mile drive to Norton St. Phillip. Monmouth Lodge is 250 yards past The George on the right.

MONMOUTH HOUSE **New**
Owners: Traudle & Leslie Graham
Norton St. Phillip, nr Bath
Somerset BA3 6LH, England
Tel: (01373) 834367, Fax: none
3 en-suite rooms
£30 per person
Open Feb to mid-Dec, Credit cards: none
Children over 4, No-smoking house

The river estuaries around Plymouth provide sheltered harbors for sailboats. Bobbing yachts fill the inlets, narrow lanes wind around wooded headlands, and the shores are lined with pretty, pastel-washed homes. Rowan Cottage has been Jeannie's home for many years and she has turned what was a pocket-sized home into a spacious abode. The large double-bedded room's ceiling rises to the rafters and has a door in the bathroom which leads into the flower-filled garden. A attractive twin-bedded room has its bathroom across the hall. Jeannie and Guy are very casual, very warm hosts who join their guests for dinner and conversation, settling them afterwards with coffee and chocolates in the large beamed sitting room with its views across the estuary. If guests prefer, they will direct them to local pubs and restaurants which serve excellent food. The Hollebones can arrange to take you sailing. Famous voyagers, such as the Pilgrim Fathers and Captain Cook, who set out on historic journeys are commemorated in nearby Plymouth. *Directions:* Leave the A38 (Exeter to Plymouth road) at the sign to Yealmpton and Ugborough. Continue to Yealmpton and take a left fork to Noss Mayo (3½ miles). Keep the river on your right all the way to Bridgend Quay, and Rowan Cottage is the first cottage on your left, up the lane.

ROWAN COTTAGE
Owners: Jeannie & Guy Hollebone
Bridgend, Noss Mayo
Plymouth
Devon PL8 1DX, England
Tel: (01752) 872714, Fax: none
3 rooms, 1 en suite
£27–£32 per person, dinner £18
Closed Christmas, Credit cards: none
Children over 11, No-smoking house
Wolsey Lodge

Jane and Robin Halfhead provide a warm welcome to their 18th-century Cotswold farmhouse set in 5 acres with magnificent views to the Marlborough Downs. The two very pretty guestrooms consist of a twin-bedded room and an airy room with a king-sized double bed, each with its private bathroom. In the morning, guests enjoy breakfast in front of the Aga at a country-pine table beneath the kitchen beam decorated with dried hops. In the evening, Jane and Robin join their guests for a drink before dinner and dine with them round the dining-room table. The tariff for dinner includes wine and a pre-dinner drink. Beyond the lovely house the garden opens up to miles of very gently rolling countryside. Guests are welcome to use the tennis court or enjoy a game of croquet on the lawn. Oaksey is on the southernmost edge of the Cotswolds and guests often visit the old market towns of Tetbury and Malmesbury with their lovely buildings and attractive shops. Farther afield lie Bath and Cheltenham. *Directions:* From Cirencester, take the A429 towards Malmesbury for 6½ miles, passing through Kemble, and turn left at the crossroads for the 2-mile drive to Oaksey. Go through the village and Oaksey Court is the second-to-last house on the right.

OAKSEY COURT
Owners: Jane & Robin Halfhead
Oaksey
Malmesbury
Wiltshire SN16 9TF, England
Tel & fax: (01666) 577265
2 rooms with private bathrooms
£28 per person, dinner £18, Credit cards: none
Closed Christmas & New Year
Children over 10, No-smoking house
Wolsey Lodge

Lise and Michael Hilton have done the most magnificent job of converting a 17th-century barn and stable into an exquisite home. Huge timbers reach to the apex of the hayloft in the living room where high-backed sofas are drawn cozily round the fire, a baby grand piano occupies an alcove, and the room opens up to a vast billiard room which the Hiltons encourage guests to enjoy. Lovely pictures and plate collections adorn the walls and enviable antiques furnish every nook and cranny. A lovely four-poster bedroom is found up the main staircase while across the courtyard two lovely bedrooms occupy the restored carriage house. Lise and Michael are the most gracious of hosts and enjoy helping guests plan their sightseeing and dining. If you are staying during the week, be sure to make a reservation for one of Lise's delicious dinners (bring your own wine to accompany the meal). Unspoilt Suffolk villages are close at hand, Constable country is within easy reach as are Dunwich, the medieval village that has almost been claimed by the sea, the elegant seaside resort of Southwold, Minsmere Bird Reserve, and the concert hall at Snape. Sample local wines at the Bruisyard St. Peter winery in the village of Bruisyard—you may come away with a case. *Directions:* Otley is 6 miles northeast of Ipswich. With the post office on your right, Bowerfield is on your right after a quarter of a mile. Lise will mail or fax you detailed driving instructions.

BOWERFIELD HOUSE
Owners: Lise & Michael Hilton
Helmingham Road
Otley, Ipswich
Suffolk IP6 9NR, England
Tel: (01473) 890742, Fax: (01473) 890059
www.karenbrown.com/england/bowerfieldhouse.html
3 en-suite rooms
£23 per person, dinner £18.50 (not Sat or Sun)
Open Mar to Oct, Credit cards: none
Children over 12, No-smoking house

The charm of Anne and Jim O'Kane and the sparkling condition of this modern suburban home just 2 miles from the historic heart of Oxford won me over completely. Jim, with his soft Irish lilt, and Anne offer a genuine warmth of welcome and never tire of poring over maps with guests to point them in the right direction for enjoying this wonderful historic city. Everything about their bedrooms is of the highest standards: each is equipped with either a double, twin, or a double and twin beds, and shower room, and is kitted out with a small refrigerator, tea and coffee tray, biscuits, chocolates, wine glasses—everything you need to make you feel at home. I was particularly impressed by the spacious ground-floor double room (room 7) and rooms 5 and 1 which contain both a double and a single bed. Jim is especially proud that Cotswold House is included in an Inspector Morse detective book. A hearty breakfast (traditional English or vegetarian) is the only meal served. For dinner guests are directed to a local pub, The Kings, or the popular Brown's restaurant in the center of town. Leave your car in the forecourt and take the bus into town. Jim suggests that your first port of call be the Oxford Tourist Office where the informative two-hour walking tours start from. *Directions:* Cotswold House is on the left, on the A4206, Banbury Road, 2 miles from the center of Oxford.

COTSWOLD HOUSE
Owners: Anne & Jim O'Kane
363 Banbury Road
Oxford OX2 7PL, England
Tel & fax: (01865) 310558
www.karenbrown.com/england/cotswoldhouse.html
7 en-suite rooms
£27.50–£29 per person
Closed Christmas, Credit cards: none
Children over 5, No-smoking house

Jean and Jack Langton are the most delightful, attentive hosts and Jean is an accomplished cook who always offers her guests a splendid dinner, or, if they prefer a less substantial meal, supper. Jean and Jack dine with their guests around the prettily set dining-room table which overlooks their large back garden. Set in a charming countryside village, The Old Rectory began life as two tiny cottages, home to the vicar's coachman and the butler. At the turn of the century the cottages were combined and became the vicarage. Parkham's vicars liked to change residences—there are three old rectories in the village. The Langtons' home is decorated in a light, airy way and while it does not abound in antiques, there is a traditional feel to the house. The largest double bedroom overlooks the garden as does a smaller double room which has its private bathroom across the hall. Guests seek out Jean in the kitchen and chat around the Aga planning their sightseeing excursions which invariably include the Royal Horticultural Society gardens, Rosemoor in Torrington, and Marwood Hill with its national collection of astilbes. Clovelly, the famous, somewhat over-commercialized village, is a great attraction, as is the Dartington glass factory in Torrington. *Directions:* From Bideford take the A39 south to Horns Cross (Coach and Horses inn) and turn left for Parkham. Bear left by the church and left at the second turning on the right. At The Bell pub turn left and The Old Rectory is on your right halfway down the hill in Rectory Lane.

THE OLD RECTORY
Owners: Jean & Jack Langton
Parkham Nr Bideford
Devon EX39 5PL, England
Tel: (01237) 451443, Fax: none
www.karenbrown.com/england/theoldrectoryparkham.html
3 rooms, 2 en suite
£36–£39 per person, dinner £23
Closed Christmas, Credit cards: none
Children over 12, No-smoking house

Penryn is a very much a working town whose main thoroughfare, Broad Street, runs up the hill from the fishing quay. Halfway up the hill, fronting directly onto the street, you find Clare House. Built in the 17th century as an impressive gentleman's residence, it was restored several years ago by Jean and Jack Hewitt who ran the town's newsagents for many years. Jean is chatty and friendly and, while guests have their own spacious sitting room, she often whisks them to her side of the house where she and Jack join them for tea and a chat in their sitting room or in the Victorian conservatory with its hundred-year-old grapevine. Jean finds that having bed-and-breakfast guests has expanded her circle of friends from the town to the world. Bedrooms at the front of the house are particularly large: one has its shower cubicle and sink in the room and the loo across the hall while the other has its private bathroom across the hall. The third bedroom is quietly located at the back of the house and has en-suite facilities. A small refreshment room stocked with tea, coffee, soft drinks, and biscuits is located between the bedrooms. Guests often walk to the Waterfront restaurant or drive to the Pandora, an adorable, thatched inn overlooking Restronguet Creek. *Directions:* From Truro, take the A39 toward Falmouth. Follow the second signpost to Penryn and turn right at the traffic lights on the quay into Broad Street—Clare House is on the left.

CLARE HOUSE
Owners: Jean & Jack Hewitt
20 Broad Street
Penryn
Cornwall TR10 8JH, England
Tel: (01326) 373294, Fax: none
www.karenbrown.com/england/clarehouse.html
3 rooms, 1 en suite
£22–£25 per person
Closed Christmas & New Year, Credit cards: none
Children over 12, No-smoking house

Swale Cottage is down a tiny country lane on the outskirts of Penshurst. Here Cynthia Dakin spent a year converting an 18th-century barn into a pretty home. Everything is cottage-cozy with white-painted walls and black beams. Cynthia's paintings (many of them of local scenery) decorate the walls. Breakfast is the only meal served on the oak refectory table and guests often go to the George and Dragon in Speldhurst (reputedly one of England's oldest pubs) or the Castle Inn in the pretty village of Chiddingstone. Upstairs, the bedrooms are cottagey in their decor and, while the four-poster is the largest room, I preferred the smaller double with its brass-and-iron bedstead and small bathroom. A twin bedroom has its bathroom across the hall. Guests enjoy a walk across the fields to Penshurst Place with its magnificent Tudor garden. It's a ten-minute drive to Hever Castle (Anne Boleyn's childhood home) and Chartwell (Churchill's home). The information packet in the rooms contains a useful chart which outlines the prices, times, and days of opening of the 20 most popular houses, castles, and gardens in the area. *Directions:* From Tunbridge Wells take the A26 north for 2½ miles and turn left onto the B2176 to Penshurst (3 miles). Half a mile before reaching Penshurst turn left into Poundsbridge Lane and, after 100 yards, right into a narrow lane signposted Swale Cottage.

SWALE COTTAGE
Owner: Cynthia Dakin
Old Swaylands Lane
off Poundsbridge Lane
Penshurst
Kent TN11 8AH, England
Tel: (01892) 870738, Fax: none
www.karenbrown.com/england/swalecottage.html
3 rooms, 2 en suite
£26–£32 per person
Open all year, Credit cards: none
Children over 10, No-smoking house

There was a farm on this site recorded in the Domesday book of 1086, though the present farm and its outbuildings date from the 1500s. Anthony's family have farmed here for generations and, while he concentrates on all things farming, Lynne concentrates on the upscale bed and breakfast that she runs in a wing of the farmhouse and the converted barns. Her accommodation is not your typical farmhouse style: the rooms I saw were furnished with pastel-painted furniture coordinating with the draperies and bedspreads, giving a light, airy feel. Bathrooms and shower rooms are sparklingly modern and one sports a claw-foot tub and separate shower. Lynne loves to eat out and enjoys discussing dining plans with guests. She also has a folder on restaurants and traditional pubs in the area. Lynne directed us to Tencreek Farm for a scrumptious Cornish cream tea in the prettiest of gardens. If you are planning on staying for a week, consider renting the adorable little cottage for two overlooking the cow pasture. Decorated in vibrant Mediterranean colors, the cottage is excellently equipped for a romantic getaway. The idyllically pretty seaside villages of Fowey, Looe, and Polperro are great attractions as are the National Trust houses of Cotehele and Lanhydrock. *Directions:* From Looe take the A387 signposted Polperro. Before you reach Polperro, Trenderway Farm is signposted to your right.

TRENDERWAY FARM
Owners: Lynne & Anthony Tuckett
Pelynt
Polperro
Cornwall PL13 2LY, England
Tel: (01503) 272214, Fax: (01503) 272991
www.karenbrown.com/england/trenderwayfarm.html
4 en-suite rooms
£25–£30 per person
Closed Christmas, Credit cards: none
Children not accepted, No-smoking house

A humorous, tongue-in-cheek "rule" book is found in every bedroom at Bales Mead and woe betide you if you do not comply! The illustrations are drawn by Peter Clover who, with his partner Stephen Blue, runs a very tight ship in their exceptionally attractive home. Guests enjoy a sophisticated sitting room complete with log-burning fireplace and baby grand piano. Upstairs, the bedrooms are named after villages in the Porlock Vale. Selworthy is cool in lemon and blue with outstanding ocean views. Bossington is all in pink, white, and mulberry with a view of the shingle beach and distant headland. Both Selworthy and Bossington have their own private bathrooms. Allerford (a smaller room overlooking the garden and woodlands) is used in conjunction with one of the other rooms by larger parties who do not mind sharing a bathroom. Breakfast is the only meal served (promptly at 9 am)—Stephen and Peter recommend excellent local pubs and restaurants for dinner. In the '50s the house was owned by a well-known horticulturist who filled the garden with specimen plants from all over the world. Just across the lane are vast stretches of shingle beach. Bales Mead is in the hamlet of West Porlock between the pretty village of Porlock and the picturesque harbor of Porlock Weir. Rising behind the house are the vast expanses of Exmoor. *Directions:* From Minehead take the A39 to Porlock, then a right turn to Porlock Weir takes you a short distance to West Porlock, where you find Bales Mead on the left.

BALES MEAD
Owners: Stephen Blue & Peter Clover
West Porlock
Somerset TA24 8NX, England
Tel: (01643) 862565, Fax: none
www.karenbrown.com/england/balesmead.html
3 rooms, none en suite
£26 per person
Closed Christmas & New Year, Credit cards: none
Children over 14, No-smoking house

The lifeboatman has been known to deliver guests to Fortitude Cottage when there's an especially high tide. While this is an adventure for visitors, Carol takes the sea coming up the road as a natural part of living beside the harbor in Old Portsmouth. When she suspects the sea may be paying a visit, she simply removes the rugs from the tile floor in the little downstairs bedroom and mops the floor when the tide ebbs. This attractive room is decorated in pink candy stripes and has a small en-suite shower room. Curl up on the window seat in the airy upstairs sitting room and watch the Isle of Wight ferries and the fishing boats come and go. On the top floor two small pretty bedrooms have tiny en-suite shower rooms (the front room has a harbor view). For dinner, Carol makes suggestions on the pubs and restaurants within walking distance. Take the waterbus (Easter to November) across the harbor to tour Nelson's flagship, *HMS Victory*, Henry VIII's ship, *Mary Rose*, and *HMS Warrior,* an 1861 iron-clad battleship, then go on to the submarine museum. *Directions:* Exit the M27 at junction 12, signposted Portsmouth and ferries. Follow signs for the Isle of Wight car ferry through the center of the town, then look for a brown signpost (at a roundabout) to the cathedral and Old Portsmouth. Pass the cathedral and at the end of the road turn right. Fortitude Cottage is on your left.

FORTITUDE COTTAGE
Owner: Carol Harbeck
51 Broad Street
Old Portsmouth
Hampshire PO1 2JD, England
Tel & fax: (01705) 823748
www.karenbrown.com/england/fortitudecottage.html
3 en-suite rooms
£22–£23 per person
Closed Christmas, Credit cards: MC, VS
Children over 8, No-smoking house

A narrow country road runs through Nidderdale (one of Yorkshire's quietest and most attractive dales) to Ramsgill, a village of a few stone houses. The Yorke Arms is tucked next to the village green with the dale rising through stone-walled fields to the high moorlands. The hotel is full of old-world charm with its polished flagstoned hallway, snug little bar, traditional residents' lounge, and large restaurant with high-backed Windsor chairs and enormous dresser decorated with pewter and china. Bedrooms are spacious and each is accompanied by a sparkling bathroom or shower room. The two superior rooms are huge in size and sport comfortable seating areas and extra-large bathrooms. A good value for money is the package that includes dinner, bed, and breakfast (two or more nights). You can take beautiful walks from the hotel which vary in length from strolls by the nearby reservoir to day-long hikes over the moorlands. The ruin of Fountains Abbey, founded by Cistertian monks in 1132 and dissolved by Henry VIII, is an awesome sight and walking paths abound. A magnificent drive takes you from Grassington through Littondale to Malham Cove (one of Yorkshire's most celebrated natural features) and back to Grassington. Nearby Harrogate is an 18th-century spa town. *Directions:* From Ripon take the B6285 to Pateley Bridge where you turn right at the signpost for Ramsgill. Ramsgill is the first village after the reservoir.

THE YORKE ARMS
Managers: Kay & Colin MacDougall
Ramsgill by Harrogate
Yorkshire HG3 5RL, England
Tel: (01423) 755243, Fax: (01423) 755330
13 en-suite rooms
£40–£60 per person, dinner £22
Open all year, Credit cards: all major
Children welcome

The Burgoyne family were people of substance hereabouts for they secured the premier building site in this picturesque Swaledale village and built an impressive home that dwarfs the surrounding buildings. Gone are the days when one family could justify such a large home and now it's a welcoming hotel run by Derek Hickson and Peter Carwardine. Derek makes guests feel thoroughly at home while Peter makes certain that they live up to their motto, "Tis substantial happiness to eat." Peter prepares a fixed-price, four-course meal every evening with plenty of choices for each course. The handsome lounge is warmed by a log fire in winter and full of inviting books on the area. There's abundant scope for walking and driving in this rugged area using Reeth as your base, though you'll be hard pressed to find a lovelier dales view than the one from your bedroom window of stone-walled fields rising to vast moorlands (one bedroom faces the back of the house). Redmire and Marrick, being more spacious, are the premier rooms. (Plans are afootto convert Marrick to a four-poster suite.) Robes and slippers are provided for the occupants of Keld and Thwaite who have to slip across the hall to their bathrooms. Richmond with its medieval castle and the Bowes Museum, near Barnard Castle, with its fine collection of French furniture and porcelain, are added attractions. *Directions:* From Richmond take the A6108 towards Leyburn for 5 miles to the B6270 for the 5-mile drive to Reeth. The Burgoyne Hotel is on the village green.

THE BURGOYNE HOTEL
Owners: Derek Hickson & Peter Carwardine
Reeth
Yorkshire DL11 6SN, England
Tel & fax: (01748) 884292
8 rooms, 6 en suite
£37.50–£67.50 per person, dinner £23.50
Open Feb 10 to Jan 2, Credit cards: VS
Children welcome

Surrounded by 3,000 acres of woodlands, 16th-century Haye Park House has the feeling of being far from civilization, yet is only 6 miles from the center of medieval Ludlow. Hot water, central heating, and electricity are supplied by two generators and the only way you can gain access to Haye House is to phone ahead so that John can meet you at the bottom of the lane and open the gate. Like the rest of the house, the large country kitchen where you dine around the long trestle table is furnished with a mish-mash of antiques and country bygones. It's all very comfortable and quirky and (generator excluded) utterly peaceful. Broad-plank-oak floors topped with rugs are the order of the day in the attractive bedrooms. If you want a large bathroom, opt for the Shell Room with its bathroom across the hall—you will be treated to a claw-foot tub set before a tall window overlooking the meadow where fallow deer come to graze in the evening. If you tire of tramping the countryside, Ludlow is close at hand. *Directions:* Leave Ludlow over Ludford Bridge traveling south. After 1 mile turn right on the B4361 signposted Richard's Castle—in 1 mile you see Moorpark School on your left and enter a woodland. Take the second right turn at the sign "Forest Walks." Remember to call ahead from Ludlow so that John can meet you at the gate. Note: The fax does not operate at night when the generator is turned off.

HAYE PARK HOUSE
Owners: Carolyn & John Stone
Richard's Castle, Ludlow
Shropshire SY8 4ED, England
Tel & fax: (01584) 831615
3 rooms, 2 en suite
£25–£30 per person, dinner £15
Open all year, Credit cards: none
Children over 12

Whashton Springs Farm is a perfect base for exploring the Yorkshire Dales. A five-minute drive finds you at the foot of Swaledale in Richmond, with its cobbled market square and Norman castle perched high above the river. The farm is run by Gordon Turnbull and his two sons who grow corn and potatoes and run a herd of hill cows and sheep. Spring is an especially good time to visit, for the little lambs are kept close to the farm. Fairlie welcomes guests to the farmhouse and offers accommodation within the large sturdy house or in one of the delightfully private bedrooms that open directly onto the courtyard. A wing of the barn has been converted into a most attractive self-catering cottage for families who want to stay for a week. Gordon serves a Yorkshire farmhouse breakfast, giving you an opportunity to ask questions about the farm, and directs guests to local pubs and restaurants in Richmond for dinner. Within an hour you can be in Durham, York, or the Lake District. The Yorkshire Dales are on your doorstep and the North Yorkshire Moors just a half hour distant. *Directions:* From the A1, take the A6136 to Richmond. Turn right at the traffic lights signposted for Ravensworth and follow this road for 3 miles to the farm which is on your left at the bottom of a steep hill.

WHASHTON SPRINGS FARM
Owners: Fairlie & Gordon Turnbull
Richmond
Yorkshire DL11 7JS
England
Tel: (01748) 822884, Fax: (01748) 826285
www.karenbrown.com/england/whashtonspringsfarm.html
8 en-suite rooms
£21–£22 per person
Open Feb to mid-Dec, Credit cards: none
Children over 5

Few English guesthouses offer the ambiance, warmth, and welcome of Mizzards Farm, a lovely 16th-century farmhouse built of stone and brick. The setting is peaceful: the River Rother flows through the 13 acres of gardens and fields and the driveway winds through the large meadowlike front lawn past a small lake. The heart of the house, where breakfast is served, is especially inviting, with one wall filled by a massive inglenook fireplace and a staircase leading up to an open minstrels' gallery. In a newer wing, a sophisticated lounge is nicely furnished with antiques and highlighted by a grand piano. Twice a year concerts are held here. The home was previously owned by an English rock star who converted the largest bedroom into a glitzy, but fun, theatrical showplace with electric curtains operated from the bed on a grand dais and a marble bathroom featuring a double bathtub. The other two guestrooms are smaller and are pleasantly decorated in more traditional decor. Dinner is not served but there are many excellent choices of places to eat nearby. For the athletically minded, Mizzards also has a covered swimming pool for guests' use. *Directions:* From Petersfield take the A272 towards Midhurst. Turn right at the crossroads in Rogate, follow the road for half a mile, cross the narrow bridge over the river, and take the first right on the small lane up to Mizzards Farm.

MIZZARDS FARM
Owners: Harriet & Julian Francis
Rogate
Petersfield
Hampshire GU31 5HS, England
Tel: (01730) 821656, Fax: (01730) 821655
www.karenbrown.com/england/mizzardsfarm.html
3 en-suite rooms
£26–£30 per person
Closed Christmas, Credit cards: none
Children over 8, No-smoking house

Rosedale Abbey nestles in a sheltered green valley below the gently rolling moorland. High above the village lies Thorgill, a few houses strung out along a narrow road just beneath the moor. Here you find Sevenford Grange, a sturdy house built at the turn of the century for the vicar of the village church, and now a private home. Linda found it the perfect place to raise her three elder sons and when they were grown, decided with her partner Ian to open their home to guests. The three large bedrooms are delightfully furnished and each accompanied by a snug en-suite shower room. Enjoy a welcoming cup of tea and a chat in the lovely drawing room and browse through the books that highlight the many things to do in this lovely part of Yorkshire. Ride a steam train on the North Yorkshire Moors Railway, visit the vast array of stately homes, explore the lovely villages nestled beneath the moor, and visit the coastside towns of Whitby, Runswick Bay, and Robin Hoods Bay. It's walking country and just above the house you can follow the path of an old railway line that takes you on a spectacular four-hour walk along the moor with views of Rosedale valley. *Directions:* From Pickering take the A170 towards Helmsley for 3 miles, then turn right for the 7 mile drive to Rosedale. Just as you enter the village, turn sharp left and go up the hill to the White House where you turn right (signposted Thorgill). Sevenford House is the first house on your right.

SEVENFORD HOUSE **New**
Owners: Linda Sugars & Ian Thompson
Thorgill, Rosedale Abbey, nr Pickering
Yorkshire YO18 8SE, England
Tel: (01751) 417283, Fax: (01751) 417505
3 en-suite rooms
£21 per person
Closed Christmas, Credit cards: none
Children welcome, No-smoking house

This solid stone cottage in the tiny village of Rowland is home to Mary Everard and her sleek black labrador Meg. Mary returned to her home area after living in the United States for several years and converted her holiday home into an adorable little bed and breakfast. The large hall, paneled in golden oak with its matching staircase leading to the bedrooms, was once the living room of a much smaller cottage. Warmed in winter by a wood-burning stove, the hall opens up to a country-style dining room with a long polished table and a softly carpeted sitting room with an array of brass fire equipment on the hearth. At the top of the stairs two prettily decorated twin bedrooms with views across the garden share a bath/shower room (with a separate loo). Breakfast, ordered the night before, includes yogurt and stewed fruit as well as the more usual cooked fare— and bread is always homemade. The nearby Peak District National Park is a walker's paradise and the countryside offers picturesque walled fields and sturdy stone villages, highlighted in the summer when the villagers decorate their wells with floral designs. Also in the vicinity are Bakewell with its antique and tea shops and Monday market, Chatsworth House, and medieval Haddon Hall. *Directions:* Leave Bakewell over the bridge and follow the Hathersage road to Hassop. At Hassop, turn left up the hill for Rowland. After half a mile turn right: Holly Cottage is on the right after two sharp bends.

HOLLY COTTAGE
Owner: Mary Everard
Rowland, Bakewell
Derbyshire DE45 1NR, England
Tel: (01629) 640624, Fax: none
www.karenbrown.com/england/hollycottage.html
2 rooms, neither en suite
£20–£25 per person, dinner £12
Closed Nov & Dec, Credit cards: none
Children welcome
No-smoking house

The Roseland Peninsula is one of Cornwall's loveliest areas, a maze of meandering narrow lanes, quaint villages, and exquisite coastal scenery. Set almost in the center of the peninsula you find one of Cornwall's loveliest homes, Crugsillick, a Queen Anne manor house extended in 1710 from an Elizabethan farmhouse, the beautiful home of Rosemary and Oliver Barstow. Guests help themselves to very reasonably priced drinks in the gracious drawing room whose lovely plasterwork ceiling was created by captive French prisoners of the Napoleonic wars. The Barstows often join their guests for dinner. The yellow bedroom is very spacious and its king-sized bed can be made into twins. The pink room has a queen-sized bed and its bathroom across the hall, while the blue (decorated in yellow) room has a twin beds and a small shower room. Guests often walk to the beach via a narrow smugglers' lane and enjoy walks along the coast. Gardens abound, the most popular being The Lost Gardens of Heligan, a recently restored garden which had been abandoned for many years. *Directions:* From St. Austell take the B3287 signposted St. Mawes to Tregony where you turn left on the B3275 through Ruan High Lanes. After ¼ mile turn left for Veryan and enter Crugsillick through the third white gate on your right over a cattle grid.

CRUGSILLICK MANOR
Owners: Rosemary & Oliver Barstow
Ruan High Lanes
Cornwall TR2 5LJ, England
Tel: (01872) 501214, Fax: (01872) 501228
E-mail: 106366.745@compuserve.com
www.karenbrown.com/england/crugsillickmanor.html
3 rooms, 2 en suite
£40–£48 per person, dinner £25
Closed Christmas & New Year, Credit cards: MC, VS
Children over 12
Wolsey Lodge

Rye, a busy port in medieval times, has become marooned 2 miles inland since the sea receded. Once the haunt of smugglers who climbed the narrow cobbled streets laden with booty from France, Rye is now a picturesque town which invites tourists to walk its cobbled lanes. On Rye's most historic street, Jeake's House dates back to 1690 when it was built by Samuel Jeake as a wool storehouse (wool was smuggled to France while brandy, lace, and salt were brought into England). From the street you enter a small reception area which leads to a Victorian parlor and bar which opens up to a large galleried hall, now the dining room, where a roaring log fire blazes in winter. At some point in its history the house was owned by the Baptist Church who built this room as a chapel. From the spacious attic bedroom to the romantic four-poster room and the snug single, no two rooms are alike. All are most attractively decorated and furnished with antiques in keeping with the historical mood of the house. All offer modern amenities such as tea-making trays, television, and telephone and all but two have en-suite bathrooms. Within easy driving distance are Winchelsea, Battle Abbey (built on the site of the Battle of Hastings in 1066), Bodiam Castle, and Sissinghurst Gardens. *Directions:* Rye is between Folkestone and Hastings on the A259. Mermaid Street is the town's main street—Jeake's House is near the Mermaid Inn.

JEAKE'S HOUSE
Owners: Jenny & Francis Hadfield
Mermaid Street, Rye
East Sussex TN31 7ET, England
Tel: (01797) 222828, Fax: (01797) 222623
E-mail: jeakeshouse@btinternet.com
www.karenbrown.com/england/jeakeshouse.html
12 rooms, 10 en suite
£22.50–£31.50 per person
Open all year, Credit cards: all major
Children welcome

Rye is one of England's most enchanting towns and Little Orchard House is one of Rye's most engaging small bed and breakfasts. The location is ideal, right in the heart of town on a small lane leading off Mermaid Street. Don't miss the inn's discreet sign. An archway frames a most inviting little courtyard faced by a pretty cottage with a red-colored door. Inside there is no formal reception area: registration takes place in the cozy, country-style kitchen which opens onto a very large old-fashioned walled garden. In one corner rises a red-brick tower, once used by smugglers to signal if the coast was clear. Bedrooms are attractive: Lloyd George is masculine and gracious, the four-poster Garden Room romantic, and the Hayloft cottagey with pine and wicker. The very friendly owners, Sara and Robert, are very involved in the management of their bed and breakfast and personally see that each guest is made welcome and pampered. To learn more about Rye's fascinating history, attend the sound and light show at the Rye Town Model, then set out to explore with a walking tour of the town. *Directions:* Follow signs to the town center and enter via the old Landgate Arch. West Street is the third street on the left off the High Street (ignore the "Authorized traffic only" signs).

LITTLE ORCHARD HOUSE
Owners: Sara Brinkhurst & Robert Bird
West Street
Rye
East Sussex TN31 7ES, England
Tel: (01797) 223831, Fax: none
www.karenbrown.com/england/littleorchardhouse.html
3 en-suite rooms
£30–£42 per person
Open all year, Credit cards: MC, VS
Children over 12

Atop the quaint cobbled streets of Rye is the ancient church and churchyard of St. Mary's, surrounded by a square of delightful old houses. Fortunately for visitors to this picturesque town, one of these, The Old Vicarage (a dusty-pink Georgian house with white trim and twin chimneys), is run as a guesthouse by a delightful young couple, Julia and Paul Masters. You can be certain of a proper cuppa here as Julia is a tea-blender and has devised a special blend of tea for her guests. Since Julia and Paul bought The Old Vicarage, they have been constantly upgrading and refurbishing the rooms. All of the guestrooms are decorated with Laura Ashley fabrics: two have contemporary four-poster beds and one has a coronet-style draped headboard. Each of the rooms has color television, hairdryer, and tea tray. There are also some small rooms tucked under the eaves on the top floor. The garden suite, a large family room with a sitting area, is below stairs. The ambiance throughout this bed and breakfast is one of homey comfort. Overnight parking is available in a small private car park nearby. If you write ahead, the Masters will send you a brochure with a map on just how to find them amongst the maze of Rye's streets. Rye deserves a visit of several days to explore its narrow, cobbled streets, antique and craft shops, and old fortifications. *Directions:* Rye is on the A259 between Folkestone and Hastings.

THE OLD VICARAGE GUEST HOUSE
Owners: Julia & Paul Masters
66 Church Square
Rye
East Sussex TN31 7HF, England
Tel: (01797) 222119, Fax: (01797) 227466
www.karenbrown.com/england/theoldvicarageguesthouse.html
6 rooms, 5 en suite
£22–£31 per person
Closed Christmas, Credit cards: none
Children over 8

This lovely Georgian home set in 5 acres of grounds in peaceful countryside offers outstanding accommodations. Rashleigh is an enormous room, its double bed having an artfully draped bedhead matching the curtains and bedspread; Treffry has a 6-foot bed which can be two single beds; and Prideaux has a dainty white four-poster. Each bedroom has an elegant en-suite bathroom with spa bath, tea- and coffee-makings, television, telephone, and a huge umbrella for guests to use during their stay. Guests have their own entrance into a lofty hallway where double doors open up to a vast sitting room all decked out in warm shades of pale green. Beyond lies a sunny conservatory with wicker chairs and little tables set for breakfast, the only meal served. Candid reviews of local restaurants enable guests to decide where they would like to eat, with choices ranging from formal restaurants to a pub on the beach in a smugglers' cove. Outside are vast lawns, a swimming pool, a hot tub, and a paved terrace with spectacular views across rolling countryside. Local attractions include the picturesque town of Fowey, the fishing village of Mevagissey, and National Trust properties such as Lanhydrock. *Directions:* Pass over the Tamar Bridge into Cornwall and follow signs to Liskeard. Take the A390 (St. Austell turnoff), following it through Lostwithiel and into St. Blazey. Cross the railway lines and opposite the Jet garage turn right into Prideaux Road, following it up the hill to Nanscawen on your right.

NANSCAWEN HOUSE
Owners: Janet & Keith Martin
Prideaux Road, St. Blazey, Par
Cornwall PL24 2SR, England
Tel & fax: (01726) 814488
www.karenbrown.com/england/nanscawenhouse.html
3 en-suite rooms
£34–£39 per person
Closed Christmas, Credit cards: MC, VS
Children over 12, No-smoking house

Breathtaking, panoramic views of the Wye Valley open up from Cinderhill House, a pink-washed cottage whose core dates back to the 14th century with additions over the years. Gillie is a warm and friendly hostess who enjoys welcoming guests to her lovely home. Bedrooms in the main house are very prettily decorated and all have tea and coffee trays. An additional attic room with twin beds and a crib is reserved for children so that parents can put their children to bed and go downstairs for dinner. Since my visit Gillie has been busy with the conversion of outbuildings to self-catering accommodation or to be used as extra guestrooms for the house. Two of these rooms have four-poster beds and one self-catering unit has been specially equipped to accommodate wheelchairs. Breakfast is a treat: fruit compotes and cold cereals are followed by hot dishes such as fresh salmon fishcakes and herb omelets, yet Gillie considers dinner her forte! On chilly evenings a crackling log fire invites guests into the large sitting room to enjoy a drink before dinner. A large ground-floor room is equipped with table tennis and darts. Apart from enjoying the peace and quiet of the Wye Valley and the Forest of Dean, guests venture farther afield to Bristol, Cardiff, Gloucester, Cheltenham, Bath, and Hereford. *Directions:* Take the M4 from Bristol towards Chepstow over the old Severn Bridge using the M48 and take exit 22 for Monmouth. Take the A466 for 10 miles, then turn right over the Bigsweir Bridge for St. Briavels. Follow the road up and the house is on the left just before the castle.

CINDERHILL HOUSE
Owner: Gillie Peacock
St. Briavels
Gloucestershire GL15 6RH, England
Tel: (01594) 530393, Fax: (01594) 530098
5 en-suite rooms
£27–£35 per person, dinner £18
Closed Christmas, Credit cards: none
Children welcome

Tim knows how to look after guests: for many years he was the manager (and one of the owners) of Number Sixteen, one of London's splendid little townhouse hotels. After selling his share of the hotel, he came back to his native Devon to run Parford Well. Set within a walled garden, the comfortable house is totally dedicated to guest accommodation while Tim lives in the tiny adjoining cottage. Sink into the oh-so-comfortable sofa in the sitting room and toast your toes before the fire. The decor is of such a high standard that, apart from the smaller proportions of the house, you would think you are in a grand country house hotel. Breakfast is the only meal served round the farmhouse table in the dining room. If you want complete seclusion, ask to eat in the tiny private dining room with grand draperies that once belonged to the Queen Mother and just enough room for a table for two. Upstairs are three delightful small bedrooms, two en suite and one with its private bathroom across the hall. Tim is an expert on where to walk, what to see, and which teashops and restaurants to frequent. He can suggest enough activities to keep you busy for a fortnight. *Directions:* From Moretonhampstead take the A382 towards Okehampton for 3 miles. Turn right at the Sandy Park crossroads towards Castle Drogo and Parford Well is 100 yards on your left.

PARFORD WELL   New
Owner: Tim Daniel
Sandy Park, nr Chagford
Devon TQ13 8JW, England
Tel: (01647) 433353, Fax: none
3 rooms, 2 en suite
£21–£23 per person
Open all year, Credit card: none
Children welcome, No-smoking house

The formal exterior of The Lodge belies the warm decor and friendly welcome which await you indoors. Sally and Roger Dixon's engaging personalities have been imprinted on their home during the three years they spent refurbishing it. Guests can enjoy croquet on the lawn, relax in the Victorian conservatory, or browse through interesting volumes in the comfortable sitting room. Sally is an excellent cook and enjoys serving elaborate dinners in the attractive dining room—the wine list offers a wide selection. The large principal bedroom has a roomy en-suite bathroom while an equally large blue and yellow double/twin-bedded room has its own private bathroom. The snug single bedroom also enjoys an en-suite bathroom. Nearby Norwich is rich in historic treasures including a beautiful Norman cathedral topped by a 15th-century spire. The castle, built by one of William the Conqueror's supporters, is now the Castle Museum. Between Norwich and the holiday resort of Great Yarmouth lie the Norfolk Broads, full of bird life and boating enthusiasts. *Directions:* From Norwich, take the A140 signposted for Ipswich for 6 miles, through the village of Newton Flotman which merges into Saxlingham Thorpe. With Duffields Mill on your right, turn left into Cargate Lane signposted Saxlingham Nethergate, and The Lodge is the second driveway on your left.

THE LODGE
Owners: Sally & Roger Dixon
Cargate Lane
Saxlingham Thorpe
Norwich
Norfolk NR15 1TU, England
Tel: (01508) 471422, Fax: (01508) 471682
www.karenbrown.com/england/thelodge.html
3 rooms, 2 en suite
£28–£30 per person, dinner £18.50
Closed Christmas, Credit cards: none
Children over 12

This Suffolk farmhouse stands amidst fields and woods in a quiet country location where for over 400 years it was a working farm. Hostess Mary's caring personality is evident in the quiet, warm way she treats her guests. Her welcome is seconded by handsome, tail-wagging dogs Jack, Bella, and Lizzie. Families with children are welcome here, though parents must supervise young ones on the narrow spiral staircase. Mary's old paintings, antique furniture, and books galore fit happily into this mellow, beamed house. Pink-toned armchairs and a long sofa border an Oriental carpet in front of the open log fire in the living room. The food served in the book-lined dining room is excellent: a typical meal might be asparagus and salmon mousse, lamb chops with fresh vegetables and new potatoes, and a choice of desserts. The large principal bedroom has a bathroom en suite while three smaller bedrooms share a bathroom and an additional loo (with a maximum of six guests at a time, the facilities are never overtaxed). Nearby are Blythburgh with its 15th-century church, Dunwich, the medieval village almost claimed by the sea, Southwold, Minsmere Bird Reserve, and the concert hall at Snape. *Directions:* From Ipswich take the A12 (signposted Lowestoft). Between Yoxford and Blythburgh take the lane beside The Little Chef (on the right) and look for High Poplars on the right after 1½ miles.

HIGH POPLARS
Owner: Mary Montague
Hinton, Saxmundham
Suffolk IP17 3RJ, England
Tel: (01502) 478528 Fax: none
www.karenbrown.com/england/highpoplars.html
3 rooms, 1 en suite
£22–£24 per person, dinner £17.50
Open all year, Credit cards: none
Children welcome, No-smoking house
Wolsey Lodge

Fronting the picturesque Teign river estuary, Shaldon is a most attractive village where every Wednesday, from May to September, residents dress in 18th-century costume, stalls are set on the green, Morris dancers entertain, and docents give guided tours of the village where the early-17th-century Virginia Cottage is one of the oldest residences. Jennifer and Michael Britton sincerely welcome guests to their home. Visitors have their own sitting room where a log fire burns cheerily in the winter and plump sofas and chairs invite you to curl up with a book or enjoy an evening of television. Breakfast is the only meal served and guests usually walk or drive to the Shipwrights Arms pub or The Green Dolphin. The double room can accommodate an extra bed and enjoys views over the garden and a large bathroom. One twin-bedded room has an en-suite bathroom while another has its facilities down the hall. If the weather is warm, you can enjoy a refreshing swim in the heated pool. There are lots of National Trust properties within a 30-mile radius. *Directions:* From Exeter take the A380 towards Torquay for 3 miles to the B3192 signposted Teignmouth and Shaldon. Cross over the bridge into Shaldon, follow the main road to your right, and turn at once sharp right, signposted Ringmore. Brook Lane is the third lane on the left and Virginia Cottage is on the right.

VIRGINIA COTTAGE
Owners: Jennifer & Michael Britton
Brook Lane
Shaldon
Devon TQ14 0HL, England
Tel & fax: (01626) 872634
www.karenbrown.com/england/virginiacottage.html
3 rooms, 2 en suite
£22–£24 per person
Open Mar to Dec, Credit cards: none
Children over 12, No-smoking house

A cozy hilltop refuge from winter storms, an outstanding spring, summer, or autumn base for exploring Derbyshire by car or on foot, Dannah Farm is a delightful place for all seasons. The solid Georgian farmhouse is turned over entirely to guests, with two cozy sitting rooms furnished tastefully and delightful cottagey bedrooms. I particularly liked the three suites, two of which have their private entries from the old stableyard. One has a snug sitting room with an open-tread spiral staircase leading to the low-beamed bedroom while the other is a lofty raftered room with a four-poster bed. Another part of the old stables is a convivial bar and country-style restaurant where guests enjoy breakfast and dinner and outside guests are welcomed on Saturday evenings. Adults and children love the animals—the squeaking baby pot-bellied pigs are a great attraction. The Peak District National Park is on your doorstep full of walks, bike trails, and appealing little villages. The stately homes of Haddon Hall and Chatsworth House are well worth a visit. *Directions:* From Belper take the A517 (Ashbourne road) for 2 miles and after the Hanging Gate Inn take the next right (at the top of the hill) to Shottle (1½ miles). Go straight at the crossroads and after 200 yards turn right into Dannah Farm.

DANNAH FARM
Owners: Joan & Martin Slack
Bowmans Lane
Shottle
Belper
Derbyshire DE56 2DR, England
Tel: (01773) 550273, Fax: (01773) 550590
E-mail: dannah@demon.co.uk
www.karenbrown.com/england/dannahfarm.html
9 rooms, 8 en suite
£32–£55 per person, dinner £17–£25
Closed Christmas, Credit cards: MC, VS
Children welcome

Standing apart from the lovely village of Sinnington just beyond its ancient church, Hunters Hill, with its magnificent countryside views, was until recent times the home of the estate manager for the adjacent Sinnington Hall. Jane and John enjoy sharing their home with guests and offer two of their three bedrooms to visitors. A large twin-bedded room has a spacious bathroom separated from the bedroom by a curtained archway. Overlooking the garden and enjoying valley views, the other bedroom has its bathroom across the hall. A snug attic room is available for children. Lovely flower arrangements add to the beautiful dining, sitting, and morning room where guests enjoy breakfast and the magnificent views across the valley to the distant Howard Hills and York. Sinnington lies on the edge of the North Yorkshire Moors National Park with its vast open spaces and little villages in sheltered valleys. The area is rich in historical sites—the ruined abbey of Rievaulx, the castle at Helmsley, and the stately homes of Castle Howard and Duncombe Park. The medieval city of York is half-an-hour's drive away. *Directions:* From Pickering take the A170 (signposted Helmsley) for 4 miles to Sinnington. Turn into the village, cross the green, keeping the village hall (which stands on the green) to your right, turn first right and follow the lane up the hill, bearing right by the church along a farm track which dead-ends at Hunters Hill.

HUNTERS HILL
Owners: Jane & John Orr
Sinnington
York Y06 6SF, England
Tel: (01751) 431196, Fax: (01751) 432976
www.karenbrown.com/england/huntershill.html
3 rooms, 1 en suite
£25–£28 per person, dinner £22–£25
Open all year, Credit cards: none
Children over 12

Gardening is Jane Baldwin's passion—not only does she tend her own 2 acres of exquisite gardens, but she also organizes the National Gardens Scheme in North Yorkshire and can recommend and arrange for you to visit other lovely gardens in the area. Her late-18th-century home is large enough to provide privacy for visitors and family. Guests have their own wing with a dining room (breakfast is the only meal served) and a low-ceilinged, very comfortable sitting room. A double-bedded room has a small en-suite shower room while a more spacious twin-bedded room shares a bathroom with another small single bedroom. Jane always ensures that the bathroom is never shared by guests who are not traveling together. For dinner, guests often wander by the river and across the green to the village pub—if you want to go farther afield, Jane is happy to make recommendations. Sinnington is a lovely, very quiet village just off the main Pickering to Helmsley road, an ideal base for exploring the lovely scenery and villages of the North Yorkshire Moors and making a day trip to the coast to Staithes, Robin Hood's Bay, and Whitby with its impressive abbey ruins. If you're a stately homes person, be sure to visit nearby Castle Howard and Nunnington Hall. *Directions:* From Pickering take the A170 (signposted Helmsley) for 4 miles to Sinnington. Turn into the village, cross the river, and turn right into the lane that leads to Riverside Farm.

RIVERSIDE FARM
Owners: Jane & Bill Baldwin
Sinnington
York Y06 6RY, England
Tel & fax: (01751) 431764
www.karenbrown.com/england/riversidefarm.html
3 rooms, 1 en suite
£20 per person
Open Apr to Oct, Credit cards: none
Children over 8, No-smoking house

A maze of narrow country roads connect the tiny little villages that dot the rolling countryside just to the south of Shrewsbury. Here you find Lawley House set amongst the cluster of homes that makes up the hamlet of Smethcott. Set atop a hill, this spacious Victorian home faces glorious countryside views across a lovely garden full of old-fashioned scented roses. Jackie loves welcoming guests to her home and makes every effort to see that they are well taken care of. Relax in the spacious sitting room and adjacent conservatory that overlooks the garden and the distant Stretton hills. The bedrooms enjoy the same lovely view. One has its spacious bathroom en suite while the other has its bathroom just across the hall. Breakfast is the only meal served round the dining room table and for dinner guests often go to The Bottle and Glass, just down the lane in Picklescott, or to The Pound, a thatched pub in nearby Leebotwood. Walkers head for the Long Mynd and often take Jackie's three-hour walk that she has outlined from the house. Shrewsbury—with its winding lanes, the castle, its many museums, the market square, and its decorative black-and-white houses—is a must visit. Further afield lies Powys castle and the industrial heritage museums of Ironbridge Gorge. *Directions:* From Shrewsbury take the A49 (towards Leominster) to Dorrington where you turn right for Picklescott. After 3 miles turn left at the crossroads for Smethcott, and ½ mile on is Lawley House, a large cream house straight ahead of you in the fork of two lanes. Smethcott appears on only the most detailed of maps.

LAWLEY HOUSE   New
Owners: Jackie & Jim Scarratt
Smethcott, nr Church Stretton
Shropshire SY6 6NX, England
Tel: (01694) 751236, Fax: (01694) 751396
2 rooms, 1 en suite
£20 per person
Closed Christmas, Credit cards: none
Children welcome, No-smoking house

The Lynch Country House was built for an attorney and his bride in 1812 and was owned by their family for over a hundred years. Roy Copeland purchased the house with the intention of running a country house hotel: however, when the renovations were complete he decided that a bed and breakfast was more his cup of tea. Consequently guests get country-house-style accommodation at bed-and-breakfast prices and Roy gets time to practice his saxophone and clarinet. Roy encourages guests to enjoy the lovely gardens with their topiary hedges and lake with its resident family of black swans. Bedrooms vary in size from snug rooms under the eaves (Alderley is an especially attractive attic room) to Goldington, a large high-ceilinged room with a grand Georgian four-poster bed. Roy supplies a list of restaurants and pubs in each room along with sample menus but finds that guests usually stroll into the village to The Globe pub. Somerton, long ago the capital of Wessex, is now a substantial village with some interesting shops and pretty streets lined with old stone houses. Glastonbury, the cradle of English Christianity, and Wells with its magnificent cathedral are nearby. Bath is just under an hour away. *Directions:* From the Podimore roundabout on the A303 follow signposts for Langport and Somerton. Join the A372 and turn right after a mile signposted Somerton. Ignore the next two Somerton signs and take the third left by the dairy. Lynch Country House is at the top of the hill by the mini roundabout.

THE LYNCH COUNTRY HOUSE
Owner: Roy Copeland
4 Behind Berry, Somerton
Somerset TA11 7PD, England
Tel: (01458) 272316, Fax: (01458) 272590
www.karenbrown.com/england/thelynchcountryhouse.html
5 rooms, 4 en suite
£24.50–£32.50 per person
Open all year, Credit cards: all major
Children welcome

Only the most detailed maps pinpoint Curdon Mill in the hamlet of Vellow, but your endeavors to find this lovely valley close to the sea and near the beautiful Quantock hills are rewarded. The approach to the mill skirts Daphne and Richard Criddle's farm. A few years ago they decided to renovate the old water mill on their property, adding a lounge where guests can relax and browse through books describing sights in the area. The mill shaft hangs across the ceiling in the dining room and the award-winning restaurant is open to the public (restaurant closed Sundays). Of the six bedrooms my favorites are the Stag Room which was named because deer can sometimes be seen in the fields below the window and the Walnut Room, named for the walnut bedheads. A small swimming pool is secluded on a terrace beside the mill. Another interesting feature is that the mill is now licensed for civil marriages. This is a rural spot where you can enjoy watching the farm animals, taking walks, trout fishing, or touring nearby gardens. Exmoor National Park is close at hand and Stogumber is a good point from which to visit Bath, Wells, and Glastonbury. *Directions:* Leave the M25 at Taunton, junction 25, and take the A358 towards Williton. Do not turn left until you see Stogumber and Vellow signposted together. Curdon Mill is on a sharp right-hand bend before you reach Stogumber.

CURDON MILL
Owners: Daphne & Richard Criddle
Lower Vellow, Stogumber
Taunton
Somerset TA4 4LS, England
Tel: (01984) 656522, Fax: (01984) 656197
www.karenbrown.com/england/curdonmill.html
6 en-suite rooms
£25–£35 per person, dinner £19.50
Open all year, Credit cards: all major
Children over 10, No-smoking house

The food at The Angel Inn is outstanding and, fortunately for visitors to this pretty part of Suffolk, guests may lodge as well as dine here. When Peter Smith and Richard Wright purchased the inn in 1985, it was in a sorry state, but now its complete refurbishment has transformed it into a building with lots of charm and old-world ambiance. Guests eating in the bar (best advised to avoid the crush by arriving early or just before last orders at 9 pm) make their selection from the menu hung on the old red-brick wall above the fireplace and then settle down at one of the tables grouped under the low, beamed ceiling. Those who prefer a quieter atmosphere may elect to dine in the restaurant where tables can be reserved in either of the two dining rooms. One is a cozy room with pine paneling, the other more dramatic, with ceilings removed to expose lofty rafters. Tables are laid with linen and soft lighting adds a romantic mood. The menu offers several choices of starters and main courses including a good selection of fresh seafood. Bedrooms are pleasantly furnished and have a light, airy decor. This unspoilt region of quiet countryside offers lots of sightseeing, such as the nearby valley of the River Stour, Dedham, and Flatford Mill, all made famous by John Constable's paintings. *Directions:* Take the A134 Sudbury road from Colchester for 5 miles to Nayland, then turn right for the 2-mile drive to Stoke by Nayland.

THE ANGEL INN
Owners: Richard Wright & Peter Smith
Stoke by Nayland, Colchester
Essex CO6 4SA, England
Tel: (01206) 263245, Fax: (01206) 263373
www.karenbrown.com/england/theangelinn.html
6 en-suite rooms
£30 per person, dinner £15–£20
Closed Christmas, Credit cards: all major
Children over 10

There is a moat most of the way round Slough Court, a 14th-century fortified manor house with tiny mullioned windows set in mellow stone walls beneath a moss-covered roof. The moat encloses a garden of rolling lawns and overflowing flowerbeds, a grass tennis court, and a sheltered swimming pool. Across the drawbridge lies the farmyard full of barns and tractors, pigs and cows. Sally is the fourth generation of her family to call Slough Court home, a home which she thoroughly enjoys sharing with her guests. Opposite the great hall with its enormous fireplace is the elegant dining room, the table prettily laid for breakfast with the cereals displayed in giant glass jars. In summer breakfast is the only meal served and guests either walk to the village pub or drive to The Rising Sun in Knapp, which specializes in fresh fish cuisine. Up the narrow staircase, heavy old doors open to attractive bedrooms with tiny paned windows and exposed wall beams (two are en suite and one has its bathroom down the hall). If you are interested in farm activities, you can watch the cows being milked and discuss the finer points of raising pigs. Basket making is a traditional Somerset craft and several local farms offer demonstrations and sell baskets. Farther afield lie the towns of Glastonbury and Wells. *Directions:* From Taunton take the A358 towards Chard to the A378 where you turn left towards Langport. In 200 yards turn left onto a country lane signposted North Curry and Stoke St. Gregory. Slough Court is on the left in Slough Lane.

SLOUGH COURT
Owner: Sally Gothard
Stoke St. Gregory
Taunton
Somerset TA3 6JQ, England
Tel & fax: (01823) 490311
3 rooms, 2 en suite
£25–£27 per person
Open Mar to Nov, Credit cards: none
Children over 12

Bretton House sits beside Fosse Way, the ancient Roman road that runs straight as an arrow through the heart of the Cotswolds. Isolated from the busy thoroughfare by 2 acres of garden, Bretton House was built at the turn of the century as a rectory. The vicar certainly enjoyed an inspirational view of gently rolling Cotswold countryside from his large rambling home. Julia and Barry bought the house specifically to provide bed and breakfast—putting to good use Barry's training as a cook and his experience managing pubs and restaurants. A pretty pine dining room has little tables and chairs set before tall windows which open up to the garden and the countryside views. For relaxation there are both a smoking and non-smoking sitting room. Up the broad staircase, the bedrooms are named for their decor: Peach has a frilly four-poster, Sweet Pea has airy flowers on the fabric and wallpaper and lovely countryside views, and Fuchsia has blue-fuchsia-covered draperies and bedspreads. All have en-suite facilities. Ask to see the enormous fluffy St. Bernards, Megan and Jessie, whose home is one of the outbuildings. Bretton House provides an ideal base for exploring the Cotswolds—within an hour you can be in Stratford-upon-Avon, Warwick, or Oxford. *Directions:* From Stow-on-the-Wold, take the A429 towards Cirencester. Pass a garage on your right and a cemetery on your left, and Bretton House is on your left at the brow of the hill.

BRETTON HOUSE
Owners: Julia & Barry Allen
Fosseway
Stow-on-the-Wold
Gloucestershire GL54 1JU, England
Tel: (01451) 830388, Fax: none
www.karenbrown.com/england/brettonhouse.html
3 en-suite rooms
£22.50 per person, dinner £15
Closed Christmas, Credit cards: none
Children over 10

Alveston Cottage began life over 400 years ago as two one-up-one-down cottages by the River Avon in the heart of Stratford-upon-Avon. Victorian additions melded the tiny dwellings into one, and more recently Louise Downing has added her skills to make this unusual house into the most inviting of homes, a home she loves to share with guests. Louise is particularly proud of her art collection where each piece is done by a person she interviewed in the course of her career as a journalist with *The Times*. The living rooms are charmingly furnished with antiques and mementos of Louise's travels round the world. Upstairs, the bedrooms enjoy an uninterrupted view of the river and are particularly attractive with their white-on-white decor and lacy Victorian pillows. One has an en-suite bathroom while the other has robes provided for trotting to its private bathroom down the hall. Theater tickets can be arranged and Alveston Cottage is just a few minutes' walk from the Royal Shakespeare Theatre. All the attractions of Stratford (except Anne Hathaway's cottage) are within easy walking distance. Advance reservations are essential. *Directions:* From Oxford take the A44 to Stratford. Before crossing the bridge into town, turn right (B4086 to Wellesbourne) opposite the Forte Posthouse (Swan's Nest Hotel) and Alveston Cottage is the first house on the riverside.

ALVESTON COTTAGE
Owner: Louise Downing
Tiddington Road
Stratford-upon-Avon
Warwickshire CV37 7AE, England
Tel: (01789) 292847, Fax: none
2 rooms, 1 en suite
£32–£35 per person
Open Apr to Oct, Credit cards: none
Children not accepted, No-smoking house

Thomas Luny, the marine artist, had this home built in 1792 in the center of Teignmouth, just a short walk through narrow streets from the sheltered harbor which has a long history as a fishing and ship-building center. Now this handsome house is home to Alison and John Allan and their two children. All the rooms have an en-suite bathroom, a television, mineral water, and a lovely old sea chest. Each is decorated in a contrasting style: Chinese enjoys a peach-and-green decor and painted Oriental furniture; Clairmont is pretty in green and yellow; Luny is autumnal in beige and brown; and Bitton contemporary with its impressive four-poster bed. Breakfast is the only meal served but there is no shortage of eating places within a few minutes walk. Follow the narrow streets of old Teignmouth to the working harbor and along to the Victorian section of town with its long sandy beach, cheerful pier, and esplanade popular with the bucket-and-spade brigade. Just across the estuary lies Shaldon where every Wednesday, from May to September, residents dress in 18th-century costume. *Directions:* From Exeter take the A380 towards Torquay for 3 miles to the B3192 to Teignmouth. Turn left at the traffic lights at the bottom of the hill, then turn immediately right signposted Quays, and immediately left into Teign Street. Thomas Luny House is on your right.

THOMAS LUNY HOUSE
Owners: Alison & John Allan
Teign Street
Teignmouth
Devon TQ14 8EG, England
Tel: (01626) 772976, Fax: none
4 en-suite rooms
£25 per person
Closed Jan, Credit cards: none
Children over 12

When I saw Brattle House, clad with weatherboard and mellow Kent peg tile, it looked like an ordinary home, so I was thrilled to enter the wide pine front door and discover that the house dates back to the 1600s and is delightful in every way. The cozy, oak-beamed sitting room opens up to a conservatory where afternoon tea and breakfast are served. Glasses and ice are provided so that guests can bring their own alcohol to enjoy drinks before, during, and after dinner which is eaten by candlelight round an antique mahogany table. After the first course, Mo and Alan Rawlinson join guests for convivial evenings of dining and conversation. Up the wide staircase are some of the prettiest of rooms–two spacious front bedrooms enjoy broad window seats overlooking the fields to the distant church tower, but I must admit that my heart was won by the cozy little back bedroom with its idyllic view across the garden to open countryside. The Rawlinsons' most popular (fine-weather) excursion (apart from nearby Sissinghurst Castle and gardens) involves taking the old Kent and West Sussex steam train from Tenterden (past the house) to Northiam, then a little wooden ferry to Bodiam Castle, where you enjoy tea at Knollys before touring the castle. *Directions:* From Tenterden, take the A28 towards Hastings for a short distance, go down the hill and turn right towards Cranbrook. Brattle House is on the left after ¼ mile.

BRATTLE HOUSE
Owners: Mo & Alan Rawlinson
Watermill Bridges, Tenterden
Kent TN30 6UL, England
Tel: (01580) 763565, Fax: none
www.karenbrown.com/england/brattlehouse.html
3 en-suite rooms
£28–£30 per person, dinner £18.50
Closed mid-Ded to mid-Jan, Credit cards: none
Children over 15, No-smoking house
Wolsey Lodge

Theberton Grange has grown over the years so that you find cozy little rooms that date back to Tudor times alongside spacious, high-ceilinged Victorian rooms. Dawn and Paul purchased the house, which had been converted to a hotel, in a state of disrepair and have worked hard to restore it—the garden with its wild wooded dell and masses of spring daffodils is neat and tidy, the patio has been relaid, and the interior has been decorated. Signs of former times remain in the numbers on the bedroom doors and the fire doors which were installed without a thought to the age of the building. The most attractive guestroom is the master bedroom (1), a spacious Victorian room with views on two sides to the garden. Two of the bedrooms have their bathrooms directly across the hall. Paul has always cooked for a hobby and is quickly expanding his considerable skills. Paul and Dawn are easy going and welcoming and ready to offer advice on where to go and what to see. On the coast Aldeburgh has delightful Georgian houses and its local council still meets in the half-timbered Moot Hall (1512). At Snape Maltings a collection of red-brick granaries and old malthouses has been converted into a riverside center with interesting shops and a concert hall, home of the Aldeburgh music festival. *Directions:* From Ipswich take the A12 (Lowestoft) to Yoxford and turn right on the B1122 to Leiston. Pass through Theberton village and immediately after leaving the village turn right (signposted Kelsale)—Theberton Grange is on your left.

THEBERTON GRANGE
Owners: Dawn & Paul Rosher
Theberton near Leiston
Suffolk IP16 4RR, England
Tel & fax: (01728) 830625
7 rooms, 5 en suite
£30–£40 per person, dinner £19.50
Closed Christmas, Credit cards: all major
Children over 9, No-smoking house

After working for many years in the south of England, Pat and Ted Hesketh decided they needed a change of pace, their objective being to live in a quiet village where they could see hills. They made a perfect choice in High Green House, sitting beside the village green in the little village of Thoralby nestled in the peace and quiet of Bishopdale which connects the busier Yorkshire dales of Wharfedale and Wensleydale. Guests enjoy a comfortable sitting room with a cheery log fire on cool evenings. Pat is happy to provide a well-priced three-course dinner with a choice of starters and desserts should guests want to eat in. The largest bedroom (a double) has a spectacular view of the hillsides dotted with tiny stone barns and its private bathroom is just next door. The smaller twin-bedded room has a snug en-suite bathroom. A ground-floor bedroom with a large en-suite shower room is equipped for disabled guests. Pat and Ted are happy to assist in planning walking and driving tours through the stunning scenery made famous by the Herriot television series. To experience some magnificent scenery, take a breathtaking circular drive from Thoralby up Bishopdale, over Kidstones Pass into Wharfedale, thence by Littondale and over the fells to Malham Cove. Return either via Ribblesdale and Hawes or via Grassington. *Directions:* Turn south to Thoralby from the A684 just east of Aysgarth village. Upon entering Thoralby, High Green House is on your right next to the village shop.

HIGH GREEN HOUSE
Owners: Pat & Ted Hesketh
Thoralby, Leyburn
Yorkshire DL8 3SU, England
Tel & fax: (01969) 663420
3 rooms, 2 en suite
£24–£27.50 per person, £15.50
Open mid-Mar to Oct, Credit cards: MC, VS
Children over 10

Thornton Watlass is a delightful Wensleydale village set amongst gently rolling farmland where quiet, narrow lanes lead you to the heart of the magnificent Yorkshire Dales. How fortunate that this lovely spot offers an award-winning bed and breakfast, The Old Rectory, a substantial Georgian home decked with wisteria, roses, and jasmine just at the edge of the village green. Olivia and Richard Farnell are justifiably proud that they won the prestigious English Tourist Board "England for Excellence" award in 1992. Olivia is the talented seamstress and decorator responsible for the enviable decor of softly hued sponged walls complementing the beautiful fabrics. The premier bedroom has a spectacular, softly draped half-tester bed and en-suite bathroom. The blue double room and spacious twin, decorated in pale shades of yellow and green, share a large bathroom and a smaller shower room, ensuring that guests always have private facilities. Guests have their own immaculate sitting room where a log fire burns in the winter and they can enjoy complimentary tea and crumpets. Breakfast is the only meal served but Olivia and Richard spoil you for choice with their suggestions of restaurants and pubs. Arm yourself with one of the Farnells' driving routes that guide you through the Yorkshire Dales. *Directions:* From Bedale take the B6268 towards Masham and Thornton Watlass is signposted to your right down 2½ miles of narrow country lanes.

THE OLD RECTORY
Owners: Olivia & Richard Farnell
Thornton Watlass
Nr Masham
Yorkshire HG4 4AH, England
Tel & fax: (01677) 423456
3 rooms, 1 en suite
£37.50 per person (2-night minimum)
Open Jun to Oct, Credit cards: none
Children over 12, No-smoking house

The huge stone cheese presses in the McGinns' paddock mark the border between England and Wales, making this an ideal base for your explorations of North Wales and for visits to the walled Roman town of Chester. Valerie and John McGinn have done the most incredible job of converting what was previously a Georgian stable block into a lovely home. Guest accommodation is offered in three delightful ground-floor rooms each accompanied by a sparkling en-suite bathroom. Two bedrooms open up to private patios, while a third offers wheelchair access from the cobbled courtyard. In warmer weather, guests breakfast in the spacious conservatory whose windows open to views of the large fish pond and pretty countryside views across the ha-ha. Guests are welcome to use the sheltered tennis court or enjoy croquet on the lawn. South Cheshire is renowned for cheese making and you can visit local producers and watch cheese being made by traditional methods. *Directions:* From Chester, take the A41 towards Whitchurch. At the New Inn pub, turn right onto B5069 to Malpas. Turn left and then first right at The Crown pub towards Wrexham. After 3 miles, pass a small filling station and the red-brick wall which borders Broughton House which is on your left before you reach the signpost for Wrexham County Borough.

BROUGHTON HOUSE
Owners: Valerie & John McGinn
Threapwood, Malpas
Cheshire SY14 7AN, England
Tel: (01948) 770610, Fax: (01948) 770472
E-mail: mcginn@broughtn.u-net.com
www.karenbrown.com/england/broughtonhouse.html
3 en-suite rooms
£27–£30 per person
Closed Christmas, Credit cards: MC, VS
Children over 10, No-smoking house

From a country road just off the A1 (London to Scotland road), you sweep down a gravel driveway to Tickencote Hall, a grand, mellow-stone manor surrounded by acres of parkland backing onto the tiny village of Tickencote with its quaint stone cottages. Dating from 1705, Tickencote Hall is home to Tarn and Peter Dearden and their three grown sons. I found the drawing room and dining room to be the height of country-house elegance and the sunny bedrooms are prettily decorated in bright chintz fabrics and furnished with antique furniture—although the comfortable beds are new. The Hall is run on traditional Wolsey Lodge house-party lines, with guests gathering for drinks in the drawing room before dining together. Nearby Stamford, with its fine Georgian buildings and narrow alleyways full of interesting antique shops, pubs, and restaurants, is a "must visit." The great houses of Burghley and Belton along with Belvoir, Grimsthorpe and Rockingham castles are nearby. In summer there's open-air Shakespearean theater at nearby Tolethorpe. *Directions:* Take the A1 north to the Stamford roundabout, continue north on the A1 for 4 miles passing two left turns and the Tickencote sign, and turn left into the Texaco garage. Cross the forecourt and turn right towards Tickencote. Take Exton Road for 15 yards only—Tickencote Hall's drive is on your left, opposite a wooden bus shelter.

TICKENCOTE HALL
Owners: Tarn & Peter Dearden
Tickencote
Stamford
Lincolnshire PE9 4AE, England
Tel & fax: (01780) 765155
www.karenbrown.com/england/tickencotehall.html
4 rooms, 2 en suite
£37.50 per person, dinner £22.50
Closed Christmas, Credit cards: none
Children over 12
Wolsey Lodge

Claiming the honor of being King Arthur's legendary birthplace, the ruins of Tintagel Castle cling to a wild headland exposed to the coastal winds. It's a place of myths that attracts visitors who come to soak up its fanciful past and enjoy its rugged scenery. While the village of Tintagel is a touristy spot, just a mile away lies the quiet hamlet of Trenale, a cluster of cottages, and the delightful Trebrea Lodge. Behind the impressive, tall Georgian façade lies a much older building of cozy, comfortable rooms. Upstairs, the drawing room is full of splendid antiques but you will probably find yourself downstairs toasting your toes by the fire enveloped by a large armchair, enjoying drinks and coffee after one of Sean's delicious award-winning dinners in the paneled dining room with its views across stone-walled fields to the distant sea. We particularly enjoyed our room (4) furnished, as are all the rooms, with lovely antiques and enjoying a large bathroom; the four-poster room (1) with its ornately carved Victorian four-poster bed; and room 5, a delightful twin-bedded room with its view to the distant ocean. A tempting array of hot breakfast dishes is placed on the buffet for guests to help themselves. Walkers enjoy spectacular cliff-top walks along rugged headlands. To the north lies Clovelly. *Directions:* From Tintagel take the road towards Boscastle and at the edge of the village turn right at the contemporary-style Roman Catholic church. Turn right at the top of the lane and Trebrea Lodge is on your left.

TREBREA LODGE
Owners: John Charlick & Sean Devlin
Trenale, Tintagel
Cornwall PL34 0HR, England
Tel: (01840) 770410, Fax: (01840) 770092
www.karenbrown.com/england/trebrealodge.html
7 en-suite rooms
£39–£44 per person, dinner £21
Closed Jan 4 to Feb 13, Credit cards: all major
Children over 12

Marjorie and Euan Aitken's home is a picture-book thatched cottage in an idyllically quiet Oxfordshire village, nestled beside a duck pond with a rowboat moored beneath overhanging willows. When the Aitkens restored the cottage, they preserved all the lovely old features they uncovered: an old range and copper boiler, beams with the carpenter's identification marks, and a pump. Every room is furnished with antiques and decorated with collections of bric-a-brac and country bygones. Across the farmyard the timbered barn has been converted to provide immaculate guestrooms with modern showers, televisions, exposed beams, and displays of Marjorie's collections. I particularly enjoyed Mary (the rooms are named after royals), its corridor hung with farm implements, a Cumberland quilt decorating the bedroom wall, and its choirboy-vestments cupboard used as a closet. Breakfast is the only meal served in the country-pine breakfast room. The milking shed next door has been converted into two more en-suite ground-floor bedrooms with access for wheelchairs. Oxford colleges, less than half an hour away, are a popular sightseeing spot, as is Blenheim Palace. Nearby Waddesden Manor, the ancestral Rothschild home, has a spectacular art collection. *Directions:* Exit the M40 at junction 6 and take the B4009 to Chinnor where you turn left on the B4445 towards Thame. After 2 miles turn right to Towersey, right at the crossroads, and the farm is on your left at the end of the village.

UPPER GREEN FARM
Owners: Marjorie & Euan Aitken
Manor Road, Towersey
Oxon OX9 3QR, England
Tel: (01844) 212496, Fax: (01844) 260399
www.karenbrown.com/england/uppergreenfarm.html
10 en-suite rooms
£22.50–£30 per person
Closed Christmas, Credit cards: none
Children over 13, No-smoking house

Pat and Richard Mason transformed a tumbledown cottage and barn in an overgrown field by a stream into a delightful home facing a pretty lake with an idyllic garden full of unusual plants. The house is just as attractive inside as out. Sofas are drawn up around the wood-burning stove in the beamed sitting room. There is an en-suite double room downstairs. The two other bedrooms are adjacent to each other and a shower room that has a super-large cubicle. The three rooms handily make into a family suite. When there are two parties of guests, the large double room has the private use of the shower room while the small blue twin has the private use of an additional bathroom down the hall. Breakfast is the only meal served: guests sometimes walk to the local pub for dinner, but more often than not they drive to the Mayfly pub which offers good food and a pretty view of the River Test. One of Pat's suggested day trips is to visit the national rose collection at Mottisfont Abbey, Hilliers Arboretum, and Broadlands, the home of the late Lord Mountbatten. Salisbury and Winchester are 15 miles distant. *Directions:* From the A303, at Andover, take the A3057 (Stockbridge road) and turn first right, signposted for Upper Clatford. Take the first left, go right at the T-junction, and turn right opposite the Crook and Shears pub into a little lane which leads to Malt Cottage.

MALT COTTAGE
Owners: Pat & Richard Mason
Upper Clatford
Andover
Hampshire SP11 7QL, England
Tel: (01264) 323469, Fax: (01264) 334100
www.karenbrown.com/england/maltcottage.html
3 rooms, 1 en suite
£20–£27.50 per person
Closed Christmas, Credit cards: none
Children welcome

Upton House, a 12th-century manor house, offers a winning combination: a lovely house with country-cottage coziness, outstanding decor, treasured antiques, carefully tended, flower-filled gardens, a charming hostess, and a swimming pool. The plasterwork between the hallway and the heavily beamed dining room has been removed to reveal ornate, ancient carved beams. The round oak dining table laid with pewter plates and goblets and in the sitting room plump sofas are grouped around a massive inglenook fireplace. A private staircase leads to the Priest's Bedroom, a twin-bedded room where everything from the towels to the lovely floral curtains coordinates with the muted-green walls. Up the main staircase you find an equally lovely double-bedded room with a large luxurious bathroom. Dinner is available with advance reservations. The ancient cider press beside the swimming pool has been opened up to provide a sitting area—a perfect place to enjoy a cool drink on a warm summer evening. The Jeffersons have maps marked for exploration of the Elgar Trail, Shakespeare country, and the Cotswolds. The nearby Royal Worcester porcelain factory's seconds shop is a favorite with guests. *Directions:* Upton Snodsbury is 6 miles east of Worcester on the A422 to Stratford-upon-Avon. Turn right by the Red Lion on the B4082 towards Pershore—Upton House is by the church.

UPTON HOUSE
Owners: Angela & Hugh Jefferson
Upton Snodsbury, Worcester
Worcestershire WR7 4NR, England
Tel & fax: (01905) 381226
www.karenbrown.com/england/uptonhouse.html
2 en-suite rooms
£34 per person, dinner £25, supper £15
Closed Christmas & New Year, Credit cards: none
Children not accepted, No-smoking house
Wolsey Lodge

Corrie has the most spectacular Lake District location—just a couple of fields separate it from Ullswater with the fells rising sharply from the far shore. For many years this was Eileen Pattinson's holiday home, a converted barn complex extended to maximize and capture the spectacular views. Now Eileen and her partner Charles run Corrie on traditional Wolsey Lodge lines, sharing their lovely home with guests. The two principal bedrooms are very spacious and the smaller single room has its shower room across the hall. The garden is a delight and includes a tennis court. Guests often wander across the fields to the lake where you can swim though the water is pretty cold. Being just a ten-minute drive from the motorway, it's an ideal spot to break your journey to or from Scotland, but do extend your stay beyond one night as the area has much to recommend it besides the utter peace and quiet that you encounter at Corrie. For the energetic, the Lakeland fells offer endless opportunities ranging from strolls to serious hikes, while touring by car presents gorgeous lake and mountain vistas. *Directions:* Leave the M6 at junction 40, taking the A66 towards Keswick for ½ mile to the large roundabout. Turn left for Ullswater on the A592 and on reaching the lake, turn right, signposted Windermere, on a road tracing the lake. Continue for 2 miles, past the Brackenrigg Hotel, down to the bottom of the hill. The entrance to Corrie is opposite a junction and telephone box.

CORRIE
Owners: Eileen Pattinson & Charles Pope
Watermillock, Penrith
Cumbria CA11 0JH, England
Tel & fax: (017684) 86582
www.karenbrown.com/england/corrie.html
3 rooms, 2 en suite
£39 per person, dinner £23
Open Apr to mid-Dec, Credit cards: none
Children over 10, No-smoking house
Wolsey Lodge

Beryl, a Gothic revival mansion on 13 acres of grounds just a mile from Wells Cathedral, is a grand house full of lovely antiques and home to Holly and Eddie Nowell and their family—a home they enjoy sharing with their guests. The measure of their success is the large number of returning guests who bring their family, friends, and even dogs (provided that they are compatible with the resident chocolate labs). Lovers of elegant antiques will delight in those found in every nook and cranny of the house—Eddie is a well-known antique dealer. All the bedrooms have special features. We loved our attic room, Summer, all pretty in pink and white with daisies on the wallpaper and bedcovers, though thought it was time for some redecoration. Next door, Spring has an elegantly draped four-poster bed to leap (literally) into. Principal bedrooms are larger and grander—choose Winston if you have a passion for grand, old-fashioned, climb-into bathtubs, Butterfly if you enjoy space and want to wake up with Wells Cathedral framed in the enormous bay window. Wells is England's smallest city, with the most glorious cathedral. *Directions:* Leave or approach Wells on the B3139 in the direction of Radstock. Turn into Hawkers Lane (not Beryl Lane) opposite the BP garage. Drive to the top of the lane and continue straight into Beryl's driveway.

BERYL
Owners: Holly & Eddie Nowell
Hawkers Lane
Wells
Somerset BA5 3JP, England
Tel: (01749) 678738, Fax: (01749) 670508
www.karenbrown.com/england/beryl.html
6 en-suite rooms
£35–£42.50 per person, dinner £20
Closed Christmas, Credit cards: MC, VS
Children welcome
Wolsey Lodge

The Citadel sits like a mighty fortress on a knoll overlooking verdant countryside. As soon as you cross the threshold, you realize this is not a "castle" of drafty halls and stone chambers, but a lovely home built to a fanciful design. A spacious sitting room occupies one of the turrets and leads to the large billiard room. Sylvia and her husband, Beverley, often join guests for sherry before dinner and then guests dine together round the long dining-room table. You are welcome to bring your own wine. Up the broad staircase, two of the bedrooms occupy turrets. I particularly enjoyed the one at the front of the house with its adjacent Victorian-style bathroom with center-stage claw-foot tub. A small twin-bedded room has an en-suite shower room. The adjacent golf club is a popular venue, but the real magic of the area lies in a visit to Hawkstone Park where you follow an intricate network of pathways through woodlands and across a narrow log bridge to high cliffs, a ruined castle, mystical grotto, and giant obelisk. The Ironbridge Gorge Museums, Shrewsbury, and Chester are within an hour's drive. *Directions:* From Shrewsbury, take the A49 (north) for 12 miles, turn right for Hodnet and Weston-under-Redcastle, and The Citadel is on your right, a quarter of a mile after leaving Weston-under-Redcastle (before Hawkstone Park).

THE CITADEL
Owners: Sylvia & Beverley Griffiths
Weston-under-Redcastle
Shrewsbury
Shropshire SY4 5JY, England
Tel & fax: (01630) 685204
3 rooms, 1 en suite
£35 per person, dinner £19
Open Apr to Oct, Credit cards: none
Children over 12, No-smoking house
Wolsey Lodge

Built in 1692 Dearnford Hall is an imposing home with an impressive array of farmbuildings. When Jane came here as a young bride, her parents-in-law divided the house into two family homes. Jane and her family grew used to their "small" end of the house, so when her parents-in-law retired to a bungalow and the children left for university, thankfully for those who visit this area she decided to take guests. The builder moved in for a year, the house was redecorated and Jane opened her doors in 1995. The house is large enough that the Bebbingtons have one wing and guests have the other. Jane feels that using the house's principal rooms as guest accommodation has given it a new lease on life. Guests have a welcoming sitting room and two extremely spacious bedrooms each with a large bathroom. Bedrooms have every possible creature comfort with blissfully comfortable beds, antique furniture, and super bathrooms. A plentiful breakfast is the only meal served but Jane helps with selections from her book of pubs and restaurants. Whitchurch is a delightful little market town and just up the road lies Nantwich and Chester—perfect for antique store browsing. It's an ideal touring base for visiting Snowdonia and a vast array of castles and National Trust properties. Enjoy some outstanding fly-fishing (lessons and rods available) on The Bebbington's 15 acre trout pool. *Directions:* From Whitchurch byepass take the B5476 towards Tilstock and Wem for ¼ mile and Dearnford Hall is the second farm on the left-hand side.

DEARNFORD HALL   New
Owners: Jane & Chas Bebbington
Whitchurch, Shropshire SY13 3JJ, England
Tel: (01948) 662319, Fax: (01948) 666670
2 en-suite rooms
£25–£30 per person
Closed Christmas, Credit cards: none
Children over 12, No-smoking house

Willersey's duck pond sits on the village green overlooked by golden-stone cottages. The lane that runs beside the pub leads to The Old Rectory, sitting in a spacious garden with the 11th-century village church as its closest neighbor. The mulberry tree in the garden is reputed to have been planted in the reign of Queen Elizabeth I and still provides fruit for breakfast. Bedrooms in The Old Rectory come in all shapes and sizes, from a snug attic room where bathrobes are provided for padding across the hall to grander en-suite rooms with four-poster beds. For a family or two couples traveling together, the Bridle and Saddle rooms in the coach house have intercommunicating doors. Guestrooms are well equipped with excellent firm beds, hairdryers, and quality toiletries. Individual tables are set for breakfast. In the evening guests usually stroll down to the Bell Inn for dinner (flashlights are provided for guiding your way home). The Old Rectory is a perfect base for touring the pretty Cotswold villages and visiting manor houses and gardens. A delightful day trip takes you farther afield to Stratford-upon-Avon and Warwick Castle. *Directions:* From Broadway take the B4632 towards Stratford-upon-Avon for 1½ miles to Willersey. Turn right into Church Street at the Bell and drive to the end of the lane, which is the Rectory private car parking area.

THE OLD RECTORY
Owners: Liz & Chris Beauvoisin
Church Street
Willersey, nr Broadway
Gloucestershire WR12 7PN, England
Tel: (01386) 853729, Fax: (01386) 858061
E-mail: beauvois@btinternet.com
www.karenbrown.com/england/theoldrectorywillersey.html
8 rooms, 6 en suite
£30–£47.50 per person
Closed Christmas, Credit cards: MC, VS
Children over 8, No-smoking house

One of the attractions for garden lovers staying at Tavern House is that Westonbirt Arboretum with its 600 acres of trees is just down the road. Although the house sits right beside the A433, there is no noise problem—thick walls and double glazing do the job in the daytime and the road is quiet at night. Breakfast is the only meal served at the cottagey little tables and chairs in the dining room and guests often go to the nearby village of Sherston to the Rattlebone Inn or the Carpenters Arms for dinner. A log fire is lit in the guests' sitting room on cool evenings. All of the bedrooms are very private as each of the four rooms has its own narrow little staircase. Room 1 is especially spacious with its high, beamed ceiling rising to the rafters, a small dressing room (ideal for parking large cases), and a bathroom large enough to accommodate a bath and separate shower. Janet and Tim used to own a large hotel in Salcombe and they have applied the same professional standards to their bed and breakfast venture. Sightseeing within a 25-mile radius includes the little market town of Chipping Sodbury; Badmington House, a superb Palladian mansion; the market town of Cirencester; Bath and Cheltenham with their Regency houses; Slimbridge Wildfowl Trust; and Berkeley Castle. *Directions:* Leave the M4 at junction 18, take the A46 (Stroud, Cirencester) to the A433 towards Tetbury. Tavern House is on your right 1 mile before Westonbirt Arboretum. Park in the lane and ring the front door bell, or use the outdoor phone.

TAVERN HOUSE
Owners: Janet & Tim Tremellen
Willesley, near Tetbury
Gloucestershire GL8 8QU, England
Tel: (01666) 880444, Fax: (01666) 880254
www.karenbrown.com/england/tavernhouse.html
4 en-suite rooms
£30.50–£33 per person
Open all year, Credit cards: MC, VS
Children over 10

Set on a hill overlooking farmland stretching across Cheshire to Shropshire and North Wales, Roughlow Farm, a converted farmhouse built around 1800, is an ideal place to stay for visiting Chester. At the heart of Sally and Peter Sutcliffe's home is a blue and white farmhouse kitchen which sits between the guests' dining room and their cozy little sitting room. Upstairs are two rooms with twin beds topped with pretty quilts, one accompanied by an en-suite shower room and the other a bathroom. An outside entrance gives access to the suite which has a spacious sitting room, bedroom, and bathroom—this can be made into a two-bedroom suite by means of an interconnecting doorway with one of the bedrooms in the main house. Breakfast is usually the only meal served, though with advance notice Sally will prepare dinner for four or more guests traveling together. Nearby Chester is a great draw, while a 45-minute drive finds you at the Albert Dock in Liverpool with its splendid museums and the Liverpool branch of the Tate Gallery. Garden lovers head for Bodnant Gardens, Arley Hall, Tatton Park, and Dunham Massey. *Directions:* Tarporley is just off the A51 between Chester and Nantwich. Go up the High Street and turn right towards Utkinton for several miles to a T-junction (Willington Hall is in front of you). Turn right and then right at the first crossroads. Follow the lane up the hill and Roughlow Farm is on your right. Willington is marked as Willington Corner on maps.

ROUGHLOW FARM
Owners: Sally & Peter Sutcliffe
Chapel Lane
Willington, Tarporley
Cheshire CW6 0PG, England
Tel & fax: (01829) 751199
3 en-suite rooms
£27.50–£32.50 per person, dinner £15
Open all year, Credit cards: none
Children over 6, No-smoking house

Stratford-upon-Avon is a Mecca for visitors who come for everything associated with Shakespeare: the performances of his plays, the town's Tudor buildings, Anne Hathaway's cottage, and Mary Arden's house. Just across the garden from Mary Arden's house you find Pear Tree Cottage, home to Margaret and Ted Mander for almost forty years, a home which has been sympathetically extended to provide seven en-suite bedrooms for guests. All the rooms are delightful, though I particularly enjoyed those in the old cottage simply because they have an especially old-world feeling. Guests have an attractive small sitting room and breakfast room with little tables and chairs set in front of a dresser displaying decorative blue-and-white plates. Two modern kitchens are available for guests to prepare their picnics or suppers and there is a washing machine for those who need to do laundry. Margaret and Ted really look after guests, providing them with an excellent map of Stratford that highlights all the things to see and, most importantly, indicates where to conveniently park your car when sightseeing or going to the theater (they can help guests to obtain tickets). Another map outlines a day tour through Cotswold villages, highlighting all the gardens, villages, houses and pubs. *Directions:* From Stratford-upon-Avon take the A3400 signposted for Henley-in-Arden for 2½ miles. Turn left to Wilmcote and Pear Tree Cottage is in the center of the village.

PEAR TREE COTTAGE
Owners: Margaret & Ted Mander
Church Road
Wilmcote
Stratford-upon-Avon
Warwickshire CV37 9UX, England
Tel: (01789) 205889, Fax: (01789) 262862
www.karenbrown.com/england/peartreecottageage.html
7 en-suite rooms
£22.50 –£25 per person
Closed Christmas, Credit cards: none
Children over 3, No-smoking house

Nestled beside the baby River Isbourne on a quiet county lane just a few yards from the main street of the delightfully pretty Cotswold village of Winchcombe, Isbourne Manor House dates back to Elizabethan times, with extensive Georgian additions. From the moment you enter, you will be delighted by the attractive decor and warmth of hospitality offered by Felicity and David King. The elegant drawing room with its wood-burning fire is exclusively for guests' use. Breakfast is the only meal served round the antique refectory dining-room table, but the Kings provide an extensive list of suggested eating places in the area. Splurge and request The Sudeley Room, well worth the few additional pounds to enjoy its elegant queen-sized four-poster bed swathed with peach-colored draperies. Langley is a most attractive double-bedded room decorated in shades of cream. Under the steeply sloping eaves of the Elizabethan portion of the house you find the snug quarters offered by Beesmore whose window serves as the door onto a large rooftop terrace (bathroom down the hall). Walk to nearby Sudeley Castle, more of a stately home than a traditional castle, then set out on a day-long tour of Cotswold villages with Bourton-on-the-Water, Stow-on-the-Wold, Chipping Campden, and Broadway being popular destinations. *Directions:* Winchcombe is on the B4632 between Cheltenham and Broadway. Turn into Castle Street (in the center of the village) and Isbourne Manor House is on the left just before the little bridge.

ISBOURNE MANOR HOUSE
Owners: Felicity & David King
Castle Street
Winchcombe
Gloucestershire GL54 6JA, England
Tel & fax: (01242) 602281
www.karenbrown.com/england/isbournemanorhouse.html
3 rooms, 2 en suite
£25–£32.50 per person
Open all year, Credit cards: none
Children over 10, No-smoking house

Sudeley Lodge, built in 1760 as a grand home on the Sudeley Castle estate, sits high on a hill overlooking rolling countryside beyond its acres of gorgeous gardens. Jim grew up here and when his parents found the house too big for them, they divided it into two with Jim, Susie, and their family having the Westward wing. Susie welcomes guests with tea and cake, encouraging them to make themselves at home in the drawing room, wander round the gardens, and walk on the farm. Upstairs the two spacious bedrooms have lovely views across the garden to the countryside. Susie loves to cook and candlelit dinners are sometimes available. There is no shortage of excellent places to eat both in nearby Winchcombe and the surrounding villages. Just down the road is Sudeley Castle with its parklike setting, magnificent medieval exterior, and largely Victorianized interior. This is an ideal spot for exploring a plethora of Cotswold villages such as Broadway, Snowshill, Chipping Campden, Lower Slaughter, and Stow-on-the-Wold. *Directions:* Winchcombe is on the B4632 between Cheltenham and Broadway. Turn into Castle Street (in the center of the village) and proceed up the hill. Pass the farm buildings on the right and turn right signed Sudeley Lodge. Pass two cottages on the way to the house.

WESTWARD AT SUDELEY LODGE   New
Owners: Susie & Jim Wilson
Winchcombe
Gloucestershire GL54 5JB, England
Tel & fax: (01242) 604372
2 en-suite rooms
£32.50 per person, dinner £21
Closed Christmas, Credit cards: MC, VS
Children over 10

Winchelsea is one of the earliest examples of town planning, having been rebuilt in 1277 after being devastated by the marauding French. The hilltop site is crowned by a church and surrounded by streets of enviable houses. Among the quiet byways are two pubs, a shop, a post office, and a tea shop (the Tea Tree). Set on a cliff overlooking the marshes, the Jempsons' 18th-century home is fronted by over an acre of manicured lawns, appealing flower borders, a walled vegetable garden, and a sheltered heated swimming pool (May to September). The house is furnished with antiques and from the flagstone hallway guests have their private staircase which leads to two pretty bedrooms. As you lie in bed in the front bedroom, you have exquisite views through floor-length windows towards the distant sea. The bathroom is a few steps down the hall. The pretty twin-bedded room has a small shower room en suite. Both rooms have televisions and tea and coffee trays. Sitting rooms are reserved for family use. Breakfast is the only meal served. Cliff, the gardener, is often on hand to discuss his vegetables and flowers. Cleveland House provides a serene contrast to the bustle of nearby Rye and a base for your explorations of southern Sussex and Kent. *Directions:* From Rye take the A259 to Winchelsea (2 miles). Go up the hill, through the arch, take the first left, and Cleveland House is the first home on the left.

CLEVELAND HOUSE
Owners: Sarah & Jonathan Jempson
Winchelsea
East Sussex TN36 4EE, England
Tel & fax: (01797) 226256
2 rooms, 1 en suite
£27.50 per person
Closed Christmas & New Year
Credit cards: MC, VS
Children welcome, No-smoking house

Just beside the cathedral in a maze of little streets in the oldest part of the city you find The Saint George, a delightful little hotel converted from two tiny row houses and the adjacent shop. Graeme named his venture after his grandfather's famous grand Victorian hotel in Llandudno, where an eight-piece orchestra accompanied dinner. The "new" Saint George also boasts many interesting features—a general store and post office off the parlor, one of the oldest wall letter boxes in Britain, a location in a thoroughfare riddled with history and character, and excellent accommodation. Settle down for several days in the Old College Bakehouse, a little cottage in the garden, with its spacious sitting room and bathroom downstairs and upstairs a bedroom with tall, arched, leaded windows opening up to rooftop views. Up the hotel's narrow staircase are four large bedrooms with absolutely everything from a sumptuous bathroom to a fax or modem point beside the desk, and a snug single. Take a guided tour of this historic college city and stroll through the King's Gate and across the lawns to Winchester Cathedral with its seven chapels, medieval wall paintings, and royal tombs. *Directions:* Leave the M3 at junction 10, come down the sliproad and take Garnier Road (a small exit) from the roundabout. At the end of Garnier road turn right and The Saint George is on your right after ¾ mile just before King's Gate.

*THE SAINT GEORGE   **New***
Owners: Anne & Graeme Jameson
King's Gate
Winchester SO23 9PD, England
Tel: (01962) 853834, Fax: (01962) 854411
6 en-suite rooms
£44.75–£62.50 per person, dinner £19
Closed Christmas, Credit cards: all major
Children over 14, No-smoking house

Hawksmoor Guest House appears no different from the many other guesthouses on these well-traveled Lake District roads until one enters, sees, and appreciates the apple-pie-order of Barbara and Robert Tyson's home. The decor is not fancy or pretentious, for this is not an expensive country house hotel, but it is well maintained: Robert boasts, "If it's broken or damaged today, it will be fixed by tomorrow." The dining room is delightfully set with pink tablecloths covered with delicate lace and laid with silver service. Barbara is happy for guests to eat in or out, always willing to provide a traditional English three-course dinner. Guests have a small comfortable lounge at their disposal. The bedrooms are smallish but each is decorated with pretty flowered wallpaper with matching curtains and bedspreads, and all have en-suite bathrooms. Robert is an expert on the Lake District and even manages to suggest a sight or two to the hurried traveler who is dashing through this lovely part of England and using it as a one-night stop on the road between London and Edinburgh. He has found that these rushed travelers often return for a stay of several days. Windermere is in the heart of the busy southern Lake District, easily accessible from the M6. *Directions:* Windermere is just off the A591 Ambleside to Kendal road. Drive along New Road and look for Hawksmoor on the right just after the clock tower.

HAWKSMOOR GUEST HOUSE
Owners: Barbara & Robert Tyson
Lake Road
Windermere
Cumbria LA23 2EQ, England
Tel: (015394) 42110, Fax: none
www.karenbrown.com/england/hawksmoorguesthouse.html
10 en-suite rooms
£27–£31 per person, dinner £12
Closed Dec 1–25 & Jan 8–31, Credit cards: MC, VS
Children over 6

Just 5 miles from the Georgian splendors of Bath, Burghope Manor is the 13th-century home of Liz and John Denning. Much of the present house dates from Tudor times and Burghope has strong associations with Henry VIII's prelate Archbishop Cranmer. Liz is a vivacious person who loves meeting people from all walks of life and all over the world and enjoys sharing her lovely home with them. Guests are encouraged to make themselves at home in the large pink drawing room, though they often prefer the cozier confines of the morning room. Upstairs, the five spacious, lovely bedrooms, all equipped with color TV and tea- and coffee-making facilities, are each accompanied by an en-suite bathroom with bath and shower. For dinner, guests stroll into Winsley village to dine at the Seven Stars pub or Nightingales restaurant. If you are planning on staying a week or longer, consider renting the Dower House, a luxurious three-bedroom, three-bathroom home sitting in the grounds of Burghope Manor. There are enough activities in Bath to occupy a week, though nearby Bradford on Avon should not be missed. *Directions:* From Bath take the A36 towards Warminster for 5 miles and turn left on the B3108 signposted Winsley and Bradford on Avon. Follow the road up into the village and, immediately after passing the 30 mph signs, turn left into a small lane to Burghope Manor.

BURGHOPE MANOR
Owners: Liz & John Denning
Winsley
Bradford on Avon
Wiltshire BA15 2LA, England
Tel: (01225) 723557, Fax: (01225) 723113
www.karenbrown.com/england/burghopemanor.html
5 en-suite rooms
£35 per person
Closed Christmas & New Year, Credit cards: all major
Children over 10

The Old Wharf's idyllic setting provides an entrancing first impression. A lane leading off the main highway wends its way down to a delightful small building hugging the edge of a tiny canal. Nearby, cows graze peacefully in meadows which stretch as far as the eye can see. The enclosed front patio is ablaze with a riot of color: a luxuriant cottage garden of colorful flowers, beautifully manicured yet artfully exuberant. The side of the house that opens onto the meandering stream is laced with climbing pink roses. The spell of the initial impression remains unbroken when you go inside. Moira and David have taken an old warehouse and converted it into their home, incorporating an outstanding small bed and breakfast. The decor throughout is fresh and airy and extremely pretty. Moira has managed to cleverly combine lovely pastel fabrics with natural-wood-finish antiques to achieve a very pretty country look. Primrose has a small double-bedded bedroom and a snug sitting room with tall windows opening up to views of the river and fields. Breakfast is the only meal served. Within easy reach are the towns of the Sussex coast, Petworth House, and Arundel Castle. *Directions:* From Billingshurst take the A272 towards Petworth, cross the canal and river, and The Old Wharf is 50 yards after the river on the left.

THE OLD WHARF
Owners: Moira & David Mitchell
Wisborough Green
Billingshurst
Sussex RH14 OJG, England
Tel & fax: (01403) 784096
www.karenbrown.com/england/theoldwharf.html
4 en-suite rooms
£27.50–£35 per person
Closed Christmas & New Year
Credit cards: all major
Children over 12, No-smoking house

Woodstock huddles by the gates of Blenheim Palace, the home of the 11th Duke of Marlborough and birthplace of Sir Winston Churchill. Holmwood offers the ideal location for exploring Blenheim with its vast grounds and visiting the nearby university city of Oxford, yet it is only a 1½-hour drive from London. This golden-Cotswold-stone Queen Anne house sitting on the main village street (not the main traffic street) proudly displays the date 1710. Christina and her Italian husband Roberto have been in the hospitality industry for many years and certainly know how to please their guests. With just two deluxe suites, each occupying a complete level of the narrow townhouse, Holmwood offers spacious accommodations. On the first floor (second in America) you enter a small sitting room with two comfortable chairs and a table set before the window where you can enjoy breakfast. This leads to a large beamed bedroom with two big windows with window seats overlooking the village street and a bed that can be made up as twins or a king. The luxurious bathroom has both a shower and a tub and a door which opens onto an outside staircase leading into the back garden. Above this sits an equally lovely queen-bedded suite. *Directions:* High Street is off Oxford Street, which is the A44 Oxford to Stratford-upon-Avon road. Park in front of Holmwood to unload your suitcases and Chris or Roberto will direct you to parking.

HOLMWOOD
Owners: Christina & Roberto Gramellini
6 High Street, Woodstock
Oxfordshire OX20 1TF, England
Tel: (01993) 81226, Fax: (01993) 813233
www.karenbrown.com/england/holmwood.html
2 en-suite rooms
£32–£35 per person
Closed Jan, Credit cards: none
Children over 12, No-smoking house

The attractive market town of Shrewsbury is a 20-minute drive from the quiet countryside hamlet of Woolstaston where you find Rectory Farm, built around 1620 in traditional Shropshire style with black timbers and white walls, sitting in a pretty garden with countryside views that stretch across the plains to Wales. John Davies was born here and now he and his wife Jeanette welcome bed and breakfast guests. Several cottagey little rooms have been combined to give guests a large sitting room either side of a massive stone fireplace. Narrow stairs wind round the fireplace to a delightful twin-bedded room set under the rafters. Up the equally narrow main staircase you find two additional bedrooms: an airy twin-bedded room large enough to accommodate a comfortable chintz-covered sofa and chair and a snug double-bedded room. A small ground floor room is available for those who have difficulty with stairs. Guests breakfast together in the dining room with its carved oak paneling and for dinner often go to The Botland Lass, just down the lane in Picklescott, or The Pound, a thatched pub in nearby Leebotwood. Perched on a hill in the midst of a great loop in the River Severn, Shrewsbury beckons to visitors—explore its winding lanes, the castle, its many museums, the market square, and its decorative black-and-white houses. For a glimpse of England's industrial heritage, visit the Ironbridge Gorge Museums. *Directions:* From Shrewsbury take the A49 (towards Leominster) to Leebotwood where you turn right for Woolstaston. Rectory Farm is on your right in the center of the village.

RECTORY FARM
Owners: Jeanette & John Davies
Woolstaston, Church Stretton
Shropshire SY6 6NN, England
Tel: (01694) 751306, Fax: none
4 en-suite rooms
£21–£22 per person
Open Feb–mid Dec, Credit cards: none
Children over 12, No-smoking house

18 St. Paul's Square is one of several large Victorian terrace homes which border a grassy square down one of York's quiet side streets. From the outside, it looks just like many other houses in this up-and-coming neighborhood, but inside it is delightfully different, showcasing colorful country-Victorian decor by Ann and Mike Beaufoy. A sunny yellow hallway rises from the entry, setting the cheerful mood felt throughout the house. In the sitting room sage-green leafy wallpaper serves as a backdrop for an old gray-marble fireplace, looking much as it must have done in Victorian times, and an old country dresser displaying blue-and-white willow dishes. The bedrooms are spacious and airy. I particularly admired the double room with warm-pine furniture and a brass-and-iron bedstead covered with a patchwork bedspread. It is a ten-minute walk from St. Paul's Square to the walls which surround the historic city center. For sightseeing, after you have exhausted the many possibilities in York, there are excursions to the North York Moors and the Dales and tours of stately homes (Castle Howard is a must). *Directions:* Leave the A64, York ring road, at the A1036 in the direction of York city center (signposted York West). Pass the racecourse and when York's walls come into view, turn left on Holgate Road (A59 Harrogate). After crossing the railway tracks, look for a right turn to St. Paul's Square.

18 ST. PAUL'S SQUARE
Owners: Ann & Mike Beaufoy
18 St. Paul's Square
York Y02 4BD, England
Tel: (01904) 629884, Fax: none
www.karenbrown.com/england/stpaulssquare.html
3 rooms, 2 en suite
£35 per person, dinner £18.50
Closed Christmas, Credit cards: none
Children welcome, No-smoking house
Wolsey Lodge

Just a few yards from York's city walls, South Parade is a private cobbled street next to a very busy main road. Inside, Number 4 is a world of quiet repose where you are invited to partake of tea and hot buttered scones in the elegant drawing room. Bedrooms are all furnished to the highest standards: bathrooms are sparkling and have modern showers, brass fittings, and are well equipped with many extras. All the rooms are decorated in soft pastels, one in soft blue-grays, another in shades of peach, with matching bedspreads and drapes coordinating with the wall covering. On the top floor, a larger room with a sitting area and writing desk gives guests lots of room for relaxation should they prefer the privacy of their room to the drawing room. Breakfast is served in the below-stairs room that was once the kitchen—breakfast orders are taken the night before and guests can order early-morning tea and a newspaper. There is an abundance of restaurants to walk to for an evening meal. Robin is full of information on York and the surrounding countryside and makes an effort to steer visitors in the right direction. Guests often enjoy a bus tour of the dales and moors. *Directions:* Leave the A64 (which forms the southern part of the York Outer Ring Road) at the A1036, in the direction of York city center (signposted York West), following signs for the racecourse. Pass the racecourse, and as you see the Odeon cinema on the left, turn right into a narrow street (next to a car showroom) which is South Parade. Parking is on the street.

4 SOUTH PARADE
Owners: Anne & Robin McClure
4 South Parade
York YO2 2BA, England
Tel & fax: (01904) 628229
www.karenbrown.com/england/southparade.html
3 en-suite rooms
£36.50–£41.50 per person
Closed Christmas, Credit cards: none
Children over 14, No-smoking house

Grasmead House was built in 1896 on a narrow strip of land sandwiched between a residential street and an ancient drovers' road leading into the walled center of York. Present owners, Stan and Sue, are locals with a warm appreciation for their historic home town and a quirky taste in decor. The guest sitting room's small bar also doubles as the reception and guests sit next to a Laurel and Hardy sculpture to watch a short video outlining York's major sights. Up the narrow staircase, each of the six bedrooms contains an antique four-poster bed—the rooms are not large and tend to be all bed. Room 2 has a delightful modern Victorian-style bathroom and the Longs plan to convert several other more dated bathrooms to this style. Breakfast is the only meal served in the little pink dining room whose window is noted for being one of the few in York that is still charged a light tax. There is no shortage of restaurants within a few minutes' walk. Guests often enjoy interesting stories in the evening when they join a guide who leads them on a ghost walk through the historic streets of this ancient city. *Directions:* Leave the A64 (which forms the southern part of the York Outer Ring Road) at the A1036, in the direction of York city center (signposted York West). Pass the racecourse on your right and just after the Mount Royal Hotel (also on the right) take the second turn right on Scarcroft Road and first right into Scarcroft Hill. Grasmead House is on the corner of Scarcroft Hill and Scarcroft Road, overlooking the park. Parking is on the street.

GRASMEAD HOUSE
Owners: Sue & Stan Long
1 Scarcroft Hill
York YO2 1DF, England
Tel & fax: (01904) 629996
6 en-suite rooms
£29–£30 per person
Open all year, Credit cards: MC, VS
Children welcome

Located on a quiet side street just a 15-minute walk from the heart of historic York, Hobbits is a delightful bed and breakfast run by Rosemary Miller and Martha Langton. This turn-of-the-century home still retains its spacious downstairs rooms, mahogany staircase, and large stained-glass hallway windows. Guests enjoy a comfortably furnished sitting room with lots of touristy brochures and interesting books on York and the surrounding villages. Breakfast is the only meal served in the dining room but there are plenty of excellent places to eat within a short walking distance. Bedrooms are not fancy—more homey than decorator perfect. Three are family rooms with a double and a twin bed, two are singles, and one a twin. Each has an en-suite bath or shower room, television, tea- and coffee-makings, and mini-bar. A ten-minute stroll finds you at York Minster, England's largest Gothic cathedral. Other attractions include the Jorvik Viking Museum, the Treasurer's House, the medieval streets of The Shambles with their inviting shops, and the castle with its adjacent museum. *Directions:* Take the A1237 (York North turnoff) from the A64 (the southern part of the York Outer Ring Road) to the A19 (signposted York City Centre). Go through the traffic lights at Clifton Green and when you see a footbridge going over the road, turn before it—this is St. Peter's Grove. Hobbits is at the end of the street on your left.

HOBBITS
Owner: Rosemary Miller
Manager: Martha Langton
9 St. Peter's Grove
York YO3 6AQ, England
Tel: (01904) 624538, Fax: (01904) 651765
www.karenbrown.com/england/hobbits.html
6 en-suite rooms
£27–£28 per person
Open all year, Credit cards: MC, VS
Children welcome

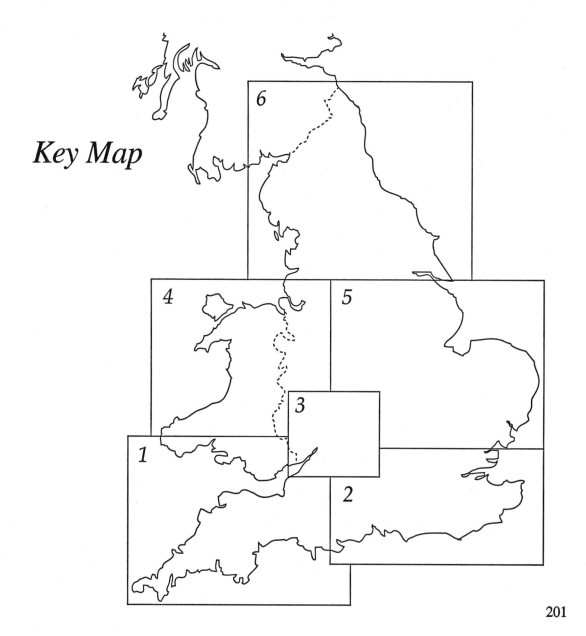

Key Map

6

4

5

3

1

2

Map 1

WALES

M50

Willersey

Broadway

○ CHELTENHAM

M5

Oaksey

Ashton Keynes

St. Briavels

Dursley

Grittleton

Nettleton

Calne

M4

BRISTOL CHANNEL

M4

Bathford

BRISTOL

BATH

Bradford on Avon

Wells

Winsley

Porlock

Glastonbury

Norton St. Philip

Dunster

Stoke St. Gregory

Lucknell Bridge

Stogumber

Somerton

Hartland

Fivehead

Marnhull

A39

Parkham

Beercrocombe

East Coker

Brampford-Speke

Affpuddle

Crackington Haven

Drewsteignton

North Bovey

Honiton

Tintagel

○ EXETER

Frampton

○

Higher Crackington

Belstone

Sandy Park

Chudleigh

Dorchester

Bucknowle

A30

Abbotsbury

Haytor Vale

Shaldon

Teignmouth

Polperro

A38

ENGLISH CHANNEL

St Blazey

Dartington

Penzance ○

Dartmouth

Penryn

Ruan High Lanes

PLYMOUTH

Noss Mayo

Goldsithney

Constantine

Lizard

Key:

- ● Places to Stay
- ○ Orientation / Sightseeing
- ✈ Airport

a	b
c	d

Quadrants

202

Map 2

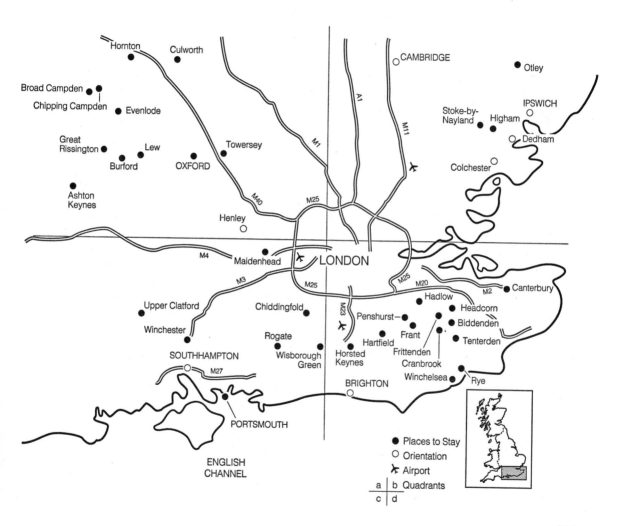

Hornton
Culworth
CAMBRIDGE
Otley
Broad Campden
IPSWICH
Chipping Campden
Evenlode
Stoke-by-Nayland
Higham
Dedham
Great Rissington
Lew
Towersey
Colchester
Burford
OXFORD
Ashton Keynes
Henley
Maidenhead
LONDON
M4
M40
M25
M1
A1
M11
M3
M25
M25
M20
M2
Canterbury
Upper Clatford
Chiddingfold
Hadlow
Headcorn
Penshurst
Biddenden
Winchester
M23
Frant
Tenterden
Rogate
Hartfield
Frittenden
SOUTHHAMPTON
Wisborough Green
Horsted Keynes
Cranbrook
Winchelsea
Rye
M27
BRIGHTON
PORTSMOUTH

ENGLISH CHANNEL

● Places to Stay
○ Orientation
✈ Airport

a	b	Quadrants
c	d

203

Map 3

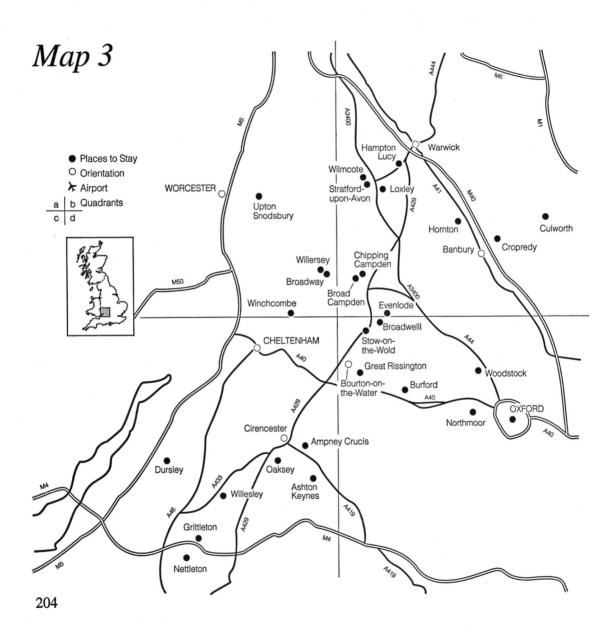

- ● Places to Stay
- ○ Orientation
- ✈ Airport

a	b
c	d

Quadrants

WORCESTER

Upton
Snodsbury

Hampton
Lucy

Warwick

Wilmcote

Stratford-
upon-Avon

Loxley

Hornton

Banbury

Cropredy

Culworth

Willersey

Chipping
Campden

Broadway

Broad
Campden

Winchcombe

Evenlode

Broadwelll

CHELTENHAM

Stow-on-
the-Wold

Great Rissington

Bourton-on-
the-Water

Burford

Woodstock

Northmoor

OXFORD

Cirencester

Ampney Crucis

Dursley

Oaksey

Ashton
Keynes

Willesley

Grittleton

Nettleton

M5

M50

M4

M5

A3400

A444

M6

M1

A40

A429

A41

M40

A429

A3400

A44

A40

A40

A429

A433

A46

A429

M4

A419

A419

204

Map 4

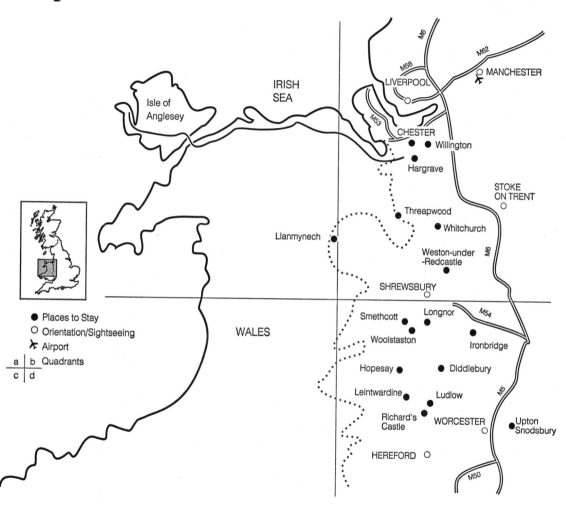

IRISH SEA

Isle of Anglesey

M6

M58

M62

LIVERPOOL

○ MANCHESTER ✈

M53

CHESTER

● ● Willington

● Hargrave

STOKE ON TRENT ○

● Threapwood

● Whitchurch

Llanmynech ●

Weston-under -Redcastle

M6

SHREWSBURY ○

WALES

Smethcott ●

● Longnor

M54

● Woolstaston

Ironbridge ●

Hopesay ●

● Diddlebury

M5

Leintwardine ●

● Ludlow

Richard's Castle ●

WORCESTER ○

● Upton Snodsbury

HEREFORD ○

M50

● Places to Stay
○ Orientation/Sightseeing
✈ Airport

a	b
c	d

Quadrants

205

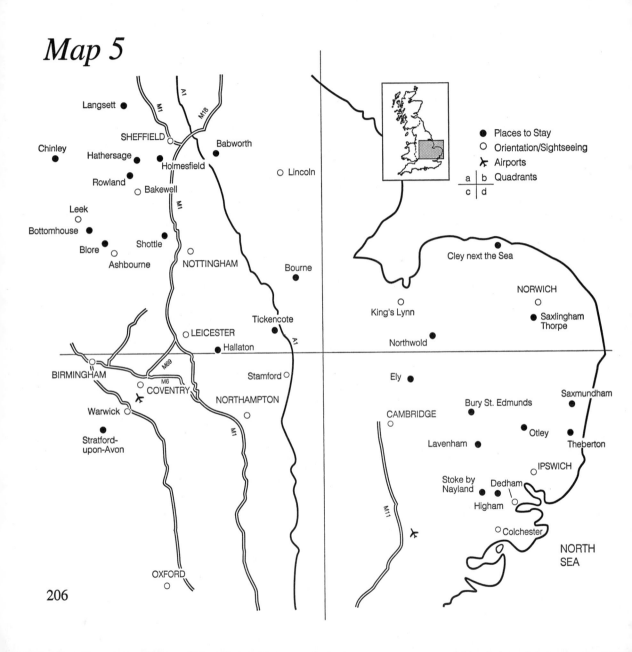

Map 5

Langsett ●

A1 M1 M18

Chinley ●

SHEFFIELD ○

Babworth ●

Hathersage ●

Holmesfield ●

Rowland ●

Bakewell ○

Lincoln ○

Leek ○

M1

Bottomhouse ●

Blore ● Shottle ●

Ashbourne ○

NOTTINGHAM ○

Bourne ●

Cley next the Sea ●

NORWICH ○

King's Lynn ○

Saxlingham Thorpe ●

Tickencote ●

LEICESTER ○

Hallaton ●

A1

Northwold ●

BIRMINGHAM ○

M69

M6

COVENTRY

Stamford ○

NORTHAMPTON ○

M1

Ely ●

CAMBRIDGE ○

Bury St. Edmunds ●

Saxmundham ●

Warwick ○

Otley ●

Theberton ●

Stratford-upon-Avon ●

Lavenham ●

IPSWICH ○

Stoke by Nayland ● Dedham ●

Higham

M11

Colchester ○

OXFORD ○

NORTH SEA

Legend

● Places to Stay
○ Orientation/Sightseeing
✈ Airports

a	b
c	d

Quadrants

Map 6

SCOTLAND

NORTH SEA

IRISH SEA

- Places to Stay
○ Orientation/Sightseeing
✈ Airports

a	b
c	d

Quadrants

Crookham

A1

NEWCASTLE UPON TYNE

Boltongale CARLISLE

Hexham

Mungrisdale

Lorton Penrith

Buttermere Valley Watermillock

M6

Little Langdale Ambleside

Windermere

Richmond Croft on Tees

Whitby

Near Sawrey

Reeth Constable Burton

Newton le Willows

Rosedale Abbey

Helm Thornton Watlass Hawnby Hutton le Hole

Kirkby Lonsdale

Thoralby

Middleham

Buckden Carlton

Sinnington

Scarborough

Capernwray

Austwick

Kettlewell Ramsgill

Malton

Bridlington

M6

Grassington

Harrogate

A1

Helperby

YORK

M58

M62

M621

LEEDS

M62

M1

Index

214   *Index*

SHARE YOUR REVIEWS WITH US

We greatly appreciate first-hand evaluations of places in our guides. Your critiques are invaluable to us. To keep current on the properties in our guides, we keep a database of readers' comments.

Please list your comments about properties you have visited. We welcome accolades, as well as criticisms.

Name of hotel or b&b _____ Town _____ Country _____
Comments:

Name of hotel or b&b _____ Town _____ Country _____
Comments:

Your name _____ Street _____ Town _____ State _____
Zip _____ Country _____ Tel _____ e-mail _____ date _____

Please send report to: Karen Brown's Guides, Post Office Box 70, San Mateo, California 94401, USA
tel: (650) 342-9117, fax: (650) 342-9153, e-mail: karen@karenbrown.com, www.karenbrown.com

SHARE YOUR REVIEWS WITH US

We greatly appreciate first-hand evaluations of places in our guides. Your critiques are invaluable to us. To keep current on the properties in our guides, we keep a database of readers' comments.

Please list your comments about properties you have visited. We welcome accolades, as well as criticisms.

Name of hotel or b&b _____ Town _____ Country _____
Comments:

Name of hotel or b&b _____ Town _____ Country _____
Comments:

Your name _____ Street _____ Town _____ State _____
Zip _____ Country _____ Tel _____ e-mail _____ date _____

Please send report to: Karen Brown's Guides, Post Office Box 70, San Mateo, California 94401, USA
tel: (650) 342-9117, fax: (650) 342-9153, e-mail: karen@karenbrown.com, www.karenbrown.com

SHARE YOUR REVIEWS WITH US

We greatly appreciate first-hand evaluations of places in our guides. Your critiques are invaluable to us. To keep current on the properties in our guides, we keep a database of readers' comments.

Please list your comments about properties you have visited. We welcome accolades, as well as criticisms.

Name of hotel or b&b _____ Town _____ Country _____
Comments:

Name of hotel or b&b _____ Town _____ Country _____
Comments:

Your name _____ Street _____ Town _____ State ____
Zip _____ Country _____ Tel _____ e-mail _____ date _____

Please send report to: Karen Brown's Guides, Post Office Box 70, San Mateo, California 94401, USA
tel: (650) 342-9117, fax: (650) 342-9153, e-mail: karen@karenbrown.com, www.karenbrown.com

SHARE YOUR REVIEWS WITH US

We greatly appreciate first-hand evaluations of places in our guides. Your critiques are invaluable to us. To keep current on the properties in our guides, we keep a database of readers' comments.

Please list your comments about properties you have visited. We welcome accolades, as well as criticisms.

Name of hotel or b&b _____ Town _____ Country _____
Comments:

Name of hotel or b&b _____ Town _____ Country _____
Comments:

Your name _____ Street _____ Town _____ State _____
Zip _____ Country _____ Tel _____ e-mail _____ date _____

Please send report to: Karen Brown's Guides, Post Office Box 70, San Mateo, California 94401, USA
tel: (650) 342-9117, fax: (650) 342-9153, e-mail: karen@karenbrown.com, www.karenbrown.com

SHARE YOUR REVIEWS WITH US

We greatly appreciate first-hand evaluations of places in our guides. Your critiques are invaluable to us. To keep current on the properties in our guides, we keep a database of readers' comments.

Please list your comments about properties you have visited. We welcome accolades, as well as criticisms.

Name of hotel or b&b _____ Town _____ Country _____

Comments:

Name of hotel or b&b _____ Town _____ Country _____

Comments:

Your name _____ Street _____ Town _____ State _____

Zip _____ Country _____ Tel _____ e-mail _____ date _____

Please send report to: Karen Brown's Guides, Post Office Box 70, San Mateo, California 94401, USA
tel: (650) 342-9117, fax: (650) 342-9153, e-mail: karen@karenbrown.com, www.karenbrown.com

SHARE YOUR REVIEWS WITH US

We greatly appreciate first-hand evaluations of places in our guides. Your critiques are invaluable to us. To keep current on the properties in our guides, we keep a database of readers' comments.

Please list your comments about properties you have visited. We welcome accolades, as well as criticisms.

Name of hotel or b&b _____ Town _____ Country _____
Comments:

Name of hotel or b&b _____ Town _____ Country _____
Comments:

Your name _____ Street _____ Town _____ State _____
Zip _____ Country _____ Tel _____ e-mail _____ date _____

Please send report to: Karen Brown's Guides, Post Office Box 70, San Mateo, California 94401, USA
tel: (650) 342-9117, fax: (650) 342-9153, e-mail: karen@karenbrown.com, www.karenbrown.com

SHARE YOUR DISCOVERIES WITH US

Outstanding properties often come from readers' discoveries. We would love to hear from you.

Please list below any hotel or bed & breakfast you discover. Tell us what you liked about the property and, if possible, please include a brochure or photographs so we can share your enthusiasm. We keep a permanent database of all of your recommendations for future use. Note: we regret we cannot return photos.

Owner _____ Hotel or B&B _____ Street _____

Town _____ Zip _____ State or Region _____ Country _____

Comments:

Your name _____ Street _____ Town _____ State _____

Zip _____ Country _____ Tel _____ e-mail _____ date _____

Please send report to: Karen Brown's Guides, Post Office Box 70, San Mateo, California 94401, USA
tel: (650) 342-9117, fax: (650) 342-9153, e-mail: karen@karenbrown.com, www.karenbrown.com

SHARE YOUR DISCOVERIES WITH US

Outstanding properties often come from readers' discoveries. We would love to hear from you.

Please list below any hotel or bed & breakfast you discover. Tell us what you liked about the property and, if possible, please include a brochure or photographs so we can share your enthusiasm. We keep a permanent database of all of your recommendations for future use. Note: we regret we cannot return photos.

Owner _____ Hotel or B&B _____ Street _____

Town _____ Zip _____ State or Region _____ Country _____

Comments:

Your name _____ Street _____ Town _____ State _____

Zip _____ Country _____ Tel _____ e-mail _____ date _____

Please send report to: Karen Brown's Guides, Post Office Box 70, San Mateo, California 94401, USA
tel: (650) 342-9117, fax: (650) 342-9153, e-mail: karen@karenbrown.com, www.karenbrown.com

SHARE YOUR DISCOVERIES WITH US

Outstanding properties often come from readers' discoveries. We would love to hear from you.

Please list below any hotel or bed & breakfast you discover. Tell us what you liked about the property and, if possible, please include a brochure or photographs so we can share your enthusiasm. We keep a permanent database of all of your recommendations for future use. Note: we regret we cannot return photos.

Owner _____ Hotel or B&B _____ Street _____
Town _____ Zip _____ State or Region _____ Country _____
Comments:

Your name _____ Street _____ Town _____ State _____
Zip _____ Country _____ Tel _____ e-mail _____ date _____

Please send report to: Karen Brown's Guides, Post Office Box 70, San Mateo, California 94401, USA
tel: (650) 342-9117, fax: (650) 342-9153, e-mail: karen@karenbrown.com, www.karenbrown.com

SHARE YOUR DISCOVERIES WITH US

Outstanding properties often come from readers' discoveries. We would love to hear from you.

Please list below any hotel or bed & breakfast you discover. Tell us what you liked about the property and, if possible, please include a brochure or photographs so we can share your enthusiasm. We keep a permanent database of all of your recommendations for future use. Note: we regret we cannot return photos.

Owner _____ Hotel or B&B _____ Street _____

Town _____ Zip _____ State or Region _____ Country _____

Comments:

Your name _____ Street _____ Town _____ State _____

Zip _____ Country _____ Tel _____ e-mail _____ date _____

Please send report to: Karen Brown's Guides, Post Office Box 70, San Mateo, California 94401, USA
tel: (650) 342-9117, fax: (650) 342-9153, e-mail: karen@karenbrown.com, www.karenbrown.com

KB Travel Service

Quality ✳ Personal Service ✳ Great Values

- Staff trained by Karen Brown to help you plan your holiday
- Special offerings on airfares to major cities in Europe
- Special prices on car rentals with free upgrades
- Countryside mini-itineraries based on Karen Brown's Guides
- Reservations for hotels, inns, and B&Bs in Karen Brown's Guides

For assistance and information on service fees contact:

KB Travel Service

16 East Third Avenue
San Mateo, California, 94401, USA

tel: 800-782-2128, fax: 650-342-2519, email: kbtravel@aol.com

---

For additional information on places in the Karen Brown's Guides, visit the following websites:
www.karenbrown.com and www.innsandouts.com

W UNITED AIRLINES

is the

Preferred Airline

of

Karen Brown's Guides

and

Karen Brown Travel Services

Seal Cove Inn

Located in the San Francisco Bay Area

Karen Brown Herbert (best known as author of the Karen Brown's guides) and her husband, Rick, have put 20 years of experience into reality and opened their own superb hideaway, Seal Cove Inn. Spectacularly set amongst wild flowers and bordered by towering cypress trees, Seal Cove Inn looks out to the distant ocean over acres of county park: an oasis where you can enjoy secluded beaches, explore tidepools, watch frolicking seals, and follow the tree-lined path that traces the windswept ocean bluffs. Country antiques, original watercolors, flower-laden cradles, rich fabrics, and the gentle ticking of grandfather clocks create the perfect ambiance for a foggy day in front of the crackling log fire. Each bedroom is its own haven with a cozy sitting area before a wood-burning fireplace and doors opening onto a private balcony or patio with views to the park and ocean. Moss Beach is a 35-minute drive south of San Francisco, 6 miles north of the picturesque town of Half Moon Bay, and a few minutes from Princeton harbor with its colorful fishing boats and restaurants. Seal Cove Inn makes a perfect base for whale-watching, salmon-fishing excursions, day trips to San Francisco, exploring the coast, or, best of all, just a romantic interlude by the sea, time to relax and be pampered. Karen and Rick look forward to the pleasure of welcoming you to their coastal hideaway.

Seal Cove Inn • 221 Cypress Avenue • Moss Beach • California • 94038 • USA
tel: (650) 728-4114, fax: (650) 728-4116, e-mail: sealcove@coastside.net, website: sealcoveinn.com

JUNE BROWN's love of travel was inspired by the *National Geographic* magazines she read as a girl in her dentist's office—so far she has visited over 40 countries. June hails from Sheffield, England and lived in Zambia and Canada before moving to northern California where she lives in San Mateo with her husband, Tony, and their children, Simon and Clare.

BARBARA TAPP, the talented artist who produces all of the hotel sketches and delightful illustrations in this guide, was raised in Australia where she studied in Sydney at the School of Interior Design. Although Barbara continues with freelance projects, she devotes much of her time to illustrating the Karen Brown guides. Barbara lives in Kensington, California, with her husband, Richard, their two sons, Jonothan and Alexander, and daughter, Georgia.

JANN POLLARD, the artist responsible for the beautiful painting on the cover of this guide, has studied art since childhood, and is well-known for her outstanding impressionistic-style watercolors which she has exhibited in numerous juried shows, winning many awards. Jann travels frequently to Europe (using Karen Brown's guides) where she loves to paint historic buildings. Jann lives in Burlingame, California, with her husband, Gene.

Travel Your Dreams • Order your Karen Brown Guides Today

Please ask in your local bookstore for Karen Brown's Guides. If the books you want are unavailable, you may order directly from the publisher. Books will be shipped immediately.

_____ *Austria: Charming Inns & Itineraries* $17.95

_____ *California: Charming Inns & Itineraries* $17.95

_____ *England: Charming Bed & Breakfasts* $16.95

_____ *England, Wales & Scotland: Charming Hotels & Itineraries* $17.95

_____ *France: Charming Bed & Breakfasts* $16.95

_____ *France: Charming Inns & Itineraries* $17.95

_____ *Germany: Charming Inns & Itineraries* $17.95

_____ *Ireland: Charming Inns & Itineraries* $17.95

_____ *Italy: Charming Bed & Breakfasts* $16.95

_____ *Italy: Charming Inns & Itineraries* $17.95

_____ *Portugal: Charming Inns & Itineraries* $17.95

_____ *Spain: Charming Inns & Itineraries* $17.95

_____ *Switzerland: Charming Inns & Itineraries* $17.95

Name _____ Street _____

Town _____ State _____ Zip _____ Tel _____ email _____

Credit Card (MasterCard or Visa) _____ Expires: _____

For orders in the USA, add $4 for the first book and $1 for each additional book for shipment. California residents add 8.25% sales tax. Overseas orders add $10 per book for airmail shipment. Indicate number of copies of each title; fax or mail form with check or credit card information to:

KAREN BROWN'S GUIDES
Post Office Box 70 • San Mateo • California • 94401 • USA
tel: (650) 342-9117, fax: (650) 342-9153, e-mail: karen@karenbrown.com

For additional information about Karen Brown's Guides, visit our website at www.karenbrown.com